Michael Foster

Chaucer's Narrators and the Rhetoric of Self-Representation

Oxford • Bern • Berlin • Bruxelles • Frankfurt am Main • New York • Wien

Bibliographic information published by Die Deutsche Bibliothek
Die Deutsche Bibliothek lists this publication in the Deutsche
Nationalbibliografie; detailed bibliographic data is available on
the Internet at ‹http://dnb.ddb.de›.

British Library Cataloguing-in-Publication Data: A catalogue record for
this book is available from The British Library.

ISBN 978-3-03911-121-3
Cover design: Mette Bundgaard, Peter Lang Ltd

© Peter Lang AG, International Academic Publishers, Bern 2008
Hochfeldstrasse 32, Postfach 746, CH-3000 Bern 9, Switzerland
info@peterlang.com, www.peterlang.com, www.peterlang.net

All rights reserved.
All parts of this publication are protected by copyright.
Any utilisation outside the strict limits of the copyright law, without the
permission of the publisher, is forbidden and liable to prosecution.
This applies in particular to reproductions, translations, microfilming,
and storage and processing in electronic retrieval systems.

Printed in Germany

Åbo Akademille,
Opetitte, että olen parempi.

Contents

Acknowledgements	9
Chapter 1 Chaucer's Voice	11
Chapter 2 The Consoler: *Book of the Duchess*	33
Chapter 3 The Scholar of Love: The Dream Visions	81
Chapter 4 The Servant of Servants: *Troilus and Criseyde*	107
Chapter 5 The Storyteller: The *Thopas-Melibee* Link	131
Chapter 6 Chaucer's Authority	157
Conclusion	175
Bibliography	179
Index	195

Acknowledgements

My love for Chaucer began in 1997 when I first heard Christopher Cannon's melodious readings of Chaucer's language, and my love for Middle English blossomed thanks to the sensitive teaching and kind encouragements of V. A. Kolve, who taught me so much. To Peter Mack I am indebted for his generous and continuous support, both as my MA supervisor and in later years. I am grateful to Joyce Coleman for her very helpful insights, which have framed my research and my understanding of aurality in late-medieval England; her influence on the pages that follow will be self-evident. A. C. Spearing has helped me formulate and refine my ideas of Chaucer's narrative voice, and I appreciate his useful criticisms of an earlier version of this text. I have benefited enormously from the insights and encouragements of Derek Pearsall, and I must also thank Dieter Mehl for his advice. I owe thanks to Thorlac Turville-Petre for his encouragement and helpful comments on portions of Chapters 5 and 6. I must also thank Brean Hammond, Jason Harding, and Matti Peikola. I am also grateful to the Donner Foundation for much needed financial support.

This research was conducted over a four-year period at Åbo Akademi University in Turku, Finland, under the supervision of Roger D. Sell as part of his "Literature as Communication" research project. All errors of fact and judgment remain the sole possession of their author.

Chapter 1
Chaucer's Voice

Chaucer's Rhetoric

Even in his lifetime, Geoffrey Chaucer's poetry and prose were read more carefully than that of other English vernacular writers. In 1385, Eustache Deschamps wrote a ballad in praise of the "Grant translateur, noble Geoffrey Chaucier", who is compared to "Socratès plains de philosophie, Seneque en meurs, Auglius en pratique, Ovides grans en ta poeterie", "Socrates full of philosophy, Seneca in morality, Aulus Gellius in practicality, great Ovid in his poetry" (1–10).[1] A year or two later, Thomas Usk has Love call Chaucer a "noble philosophical poete in Englissh" whose "goodnes of gentyl manlyche speche" makes him "passeth al other makers".[2] Similarly, in the *Prologue* to John Gower's *Confessio Amantis*, Venus declares her particular affection for Chaucer:

> And gret wel Chaucer whan ye mete,
> As mi disciple and mi poete:
> For in the floures of his youthe
> In sondri wise, as he wel couthe,
> Of Ditees and of songes glade,
> The whiche he for mi sake made,
> The lond fulfild is overal:
> Wherof to him in special
> Above alle othre I am most holde. (2941–9)[3]

---

[1] I am quoting from *Œuvres complètes de Eustache Deschamps* vol. 11, A. H. E. Queux de Saint-Hilaire (ed.). Paris: Firmin Didot, 1903.

[2] *Testament of Love* Book III, Chapter IV, edited in *Chaucerian and Other Pieces*, W. W. Skeat (ed.). Oxford: Clarendon Press, 1897: 1–145.

[3] *The English Works of John Gower*, vol. 1. G. C. Macaulay (ed.). London: EETS ES 81, 1901.

In the fifteenth century, praise of Chaucer expands. The exaltations of John Lydgate, Thomas Hoccleve, and Robert Henryson are well known, but they are not exceptional. Scribes adulated Chaucer in manuscripts.[4] Children were urged to read his poetry.[5] In light of the enthusiasm of these many responses, Derek Pearsall's characterisation of the "early-fifteenth-century cult of Chaucer"[6] seems particularly apt.

These are not praises of Chaucer the man, or of the civil servant we find in records, but of the poet, whose work moved so many of his contemporaries and near-contemporaries to hyperbole. More often than not, Chaucer is praised for his eloquence or rhetoric. For the anonymous author of the *Book of Curtesye*, Chaucer's rhetorical skill is a lesson to be learned, for it teaches how to gain the benevolence of an audience:

> O fader and founder of ornate eloquence
> That enlumened hast alle our bretayne
> To soone we loste thy laureate scyence
> O lusty lyquour of that fulsom fontayne
> O cursid deth why hast thou þat poete slayne
> I mene fader chaucer maister galfryde
> Alas the whyle that euer he from vs dyde. (330–6)
> ...
> Redeth my chylde redeth his bookes alle
> Refuseth none they ben expedyente
> Sentence or langage or bothe fynde ye shalle
> Ful delectable for that good fader mente
> Of al his purpose and his hole entente
> How to plese in euery audyence
> And in our tunge was welle of eloquence. (344–50)

Chaucer's ability to please an audience is one part of his rhetoric; his eloquent construction of melodious poetry is another. Thus John

---

4 Seth Lerer, *Chaucer and His Readers*. Princeton, NJ: Princeton University Press, 1993: 44–56.
5 See the "Book of Curtesye", 330–50, edited by Frederick J. Furnivall in *Caxton's Book of Curtesye*. London: EETS ES 3, 1868.
6 "Review of John H. Fisher, *The Importance of Chaucer*", *Speculum* 68 (1993): 760–1, at 761.

Metham wrote that "with many prouerbys hys bokys he rymyd naturally", William Caxton spoke of Chaucer as the "enbelissher of ornate eloquence in our englissh", and William Dunbar called "reverend Chaucer" the "rose of rethoris all".[7]

When studying Chaucer's narrator, twentieth and twenty-first century studies have occasionally made recourse to the rhetorical tradition. Largely beginning with John M. Manly's *Chaucer and the Rhetoricians*,[8] this trend of studying the rhetorical tradition's influence on Chaucer borrowed from many rhetorical traditions, particularly Cicero and his followers.[9] Yet James J. Murphy's criticism of this approach, based on the argument that "there is very little evidence of an active rhetorical tradition in fourteenth-century England",[10] has raised doubts, and Murphy demonstrates that the rhetorical tradition's direct influence on Chaucer is questionable. Although Chaucer shows familiarity with Vinsauf and alludes to Horace[11] and Cicero, it does not necessarily follow that these writers were major sources of inspiration. Links with other rhetoricians, either classical (most notably Aristotle) or medieval (such as Peter of Blois and John of Briggis) are still more difficult to discover. Paradoxically, this is partly due to rhetoric's widespread influence on poetry; since Chaucer was greatly influenced by figures such as Guillaume de Machaut, Guillaume de Lorris, and Jean de Meun, he could have learned the rhetorical *topoi* "from his French models without ever resorting to rhetorical treatises or the medieval manuals".[12] In other words, poetry's status in the Middle

---

7   All quoted in Derek Brewer, *Geoffrey Chaucer: The Critical Heritage Volume 1, 1385–1837*. London: Routledge, 1978. For Dunbar, Pearsall uses J. Small's edition, Edinburgh: Scottish Text Society X (1893).

8   London: British Academy, 1926. For a bibliography of such studies, see James J. Murphy, "A New Look at Chaucer and the Rhetoricians", *Review of English Studies* 14 (1964): 1–20, at 1 n.1.

9   For example, Robert O. Payne, "Chaucer and the Art of Rhetoric", in *A Companion to Chaucer Studies*, Beryl Rowland (ed.). New York: Oxford University Press, 1979: 42–64.

10 "A New Look", 2.

11 Even if he never read him. See Harriet Seibert, "Chaucer and Horace", *MLN* 31 (1916) 304–7; for a response, see C. L. Wrenn, "Chaucer's Knowledge of Horace", *Modern Language Review* 18 (1923): 286–92.

12 Murphy, "A New Look", 15.

Ages as a daughter of rhetoric made rhetoric inescapable, if not the classical and medieval rhetorical treatises themselves.

This is not to say that Chaucer did not have a rhetorical aim and did not apply the *topoi* of the rhetorical tradition to his texts, even if writers like Vinsauf did not motivate him to do so. Murphy reminds us that "there are some figures [of rhetoric] which any writer will use unconsciously",[13] so the rhetorical tradition may help us read Chaucer's poetry and identify the intended rhetorical effects of particular passages, even if it cannot help us produce stemmata of Chaucer's rhetoric.

At this point we must distinguish between rhetorical effect and stylistic construction. Aristotle defines rhetoric as "the possible means of persuasion in reference to any subject whatever";[14] accordingly, rhetoric can arouse "prejudice, compassion, anger, and similar emotions".[15] Unlike stylistic analyses that examine the qualities of an author's prosody and *ethos* to pronounce judgment on the text or its author, a rhetorical analysis engages the author's anticipation of his or her audience's responses but does not codify what those responses are supposed to be. Instead, it sheds light on how much interpretative authority authors give their audiences, and which potential responses are urged by the text's construction.

Examinations of Chaucer's rhetoric have borne much fruit in recent years, such as Arthur W. Bahr's rhetorical analysis of the narrator in *Book of the Duchess*[16] and R. J. Shoeck's reading of the ironic layering of author, audience, and characters in *Troilus and Criseyde*, which emphasises "how reciprocal are the concepts and functions of audience, subject, and speaker".[17] While Bahr's essay uncovers the awkward historical context surrounding both Chaucer and his poem, Shoeck suggests how Chaucer creates a context for *Troilus and Criseyde* that

---

13 Ibid., 15.
14 *Rhetoric* I.II (edited and translated by John Henry Freese (ed.. and trans.). Cambridge, Mass.: Harvard University Press, 1926).
15 *Rhetoric* I.I.
16 Arthur W. Bahr, "The Rhetorical Construction of Narrator and Narrative in Chaucer's the *Book of the Duchess*", *Chaucer Review* 35 (2000): 43–59.
17 "Chaucerian Irony Revisited: A Rhetorical Perspective", *Florilegium* 11 (1992): 124–41, at 127.

focuses on an active, reciprocal communication between author and audience, which in turn demands an open exchange of ideas and perspectives without the dogmatic interpretation of a singular authority. This present book is an attempt to map Chaucer's rhetorical construction of his identity as an author who presents ideas and stories and the identities of his audiences, who are invited to interpret those ideas and stories in an open, public forum. Such an imagined context, I argue, is not a fiction, but an attempt to position people – including Chaucer – in the community that his texts imply and create.[18]

Chaucer's Narrators

My choice of Chaucer's narrators as a *locus* of his rhetorical self-representation is based on the assumption that they are more than imaginative constructions, stylistic devices, and fictional characters: I would like to suggest that the narrator should be understood as a reflection of the author, and that Chaucer expected his audience to conflate the narrator with the author. This conflation in turn opens a rhetorical space that can be manipulated in many ways.

Some previous studies of Chaucer's narrator encourage such an approach, while others challenge it. The debate on Chaucer's narrator begins to a large part with George Lyman Kittredge, who invites us to read the "childlike Dreamer" of the *Book of the Duchess* as an autonomous fiction:

> This childlike Dreamer, who never reasons, but only feels and gets impressions, who never knows what anything means until he is told in the plainest language, is not Geoffrey Chaucer, the humorist and man of the world. He is a creature of the imagination, and his childlikeness is part of his dramatic character.[19]

---

18 For more on this notion of literature as community-making, see Roger D. Sell, *Literature as Communication*. Amsterdam: John Benjamins, 2000.
19 *Chaucer and His Poetry*. Cambridge, Mass.: Harvard University Press, 1920: 50.

This dramatic reading became standard throughout much of the twentieth century, largely helped by E. T. Donaldson's enormously influential article of 1954, which proclaims with relief that "Kittredge's pronouncement cleared the air, and most of us now accept the proposition that Chaucer was sophisticated as readily as we do the proposition that the whale is a mammal".[20] Donaldson extends Kittredge's argument to the narrator of the *Canterbury Tales*, who, accordingly, was "acutely unaware of the significance of what he sees, no matter how sharply he sees it".[21]

Yet Donaldson's account of the fictional narrator is not as confident as it at first appears. Donaldson distinguishes between "Chaucer the pilgrim", "Chaucer the poet", and "that Geoffrey Chaucer frequently mentioned in contemporary historical records as a distinguished civil servant, but never as a poet".[22] But he also admits that the

> fact that these are three separate entities does not, naturally, exclude the probability – or rather the certainty – that they bore a close resemblance to one another, and that, indeed, they frequently got together in the same body.[23]

Donaldson's essay, in tandem with another by him on *Troilus and Criseyde*,[24] prompted a number of studies of the narrator as a fictional character; despite their similar approach, these studies provide differing, sometimes contradictory, conclusions. Thus John M. Major, devoted to a reading of the *Canterbury Tales*-narrator as a fictional character, discovers in him "a marvelously alert, ironic, facetious master of every situation"[25] – quite unlike the bumbling figure of Kittredge! On the other side of the spectrum is Ruth Nevo, who finds in the nar-

---

20 "Chaucer the Pilgrim", *PMLA* 69 (1954): 928–36, at 929.
21 Ibid.
22 Ibid., 928.
23 Ibid.
24 "The Ending of Chaucer's *Troilus*", in *Early English and Norse Studies Presented to Hugh Smith*, Arthur Brown and Peter Foote (eds.). London: Methuen, 1963: 26–45, discussed in Chapter 4.
25 John M. Major, "The Personality of Chaucer the Pilgrim", *PMLA* 75 (1960): 160–2, at 162.

rator "the innocent, the simpleton", which allows Chaucer to accept, on the surface, the worldly values of the pilgrims.[26]

Dorothy Bethurum is more circumspect, searching for narratorial conventions in Chaucer's sources. Her study leads to the suggestion that the narrator creates a "contrast between books and experience, between the stable world of learning and the fragile world of love".[27] In *Book of the Duchess*, he is "like Conrad's Marlow, the screen through which the real emotion is filtered".[28] This stance, she suggests, becomes a perfect position for Chaucer, since it

> sets him off at a great distance from the knightly subject of his poem, the perfect lover. The effect is comic, of course, yet it provides the ideally tactful form in which a bourgeois poet may record the grief of his patron, the chief knight of the realm, for the death of his wife.[29]

Bethurum's reading is interesting, because it combines the fallible narrator theory of Donaldson with Bertrand H. Bronson's claim that fictional narrators did not exist in Chaucer's day.[30] Bronson's position is worth quoting in full:

> One figure is omnipresent in all his [Chaucer's] work, and that is himself as objectified in his various narrative writings. It is a current fashion, not to say a fad, to discuss the *persona* in works of fiction, and of late there has been a rash of talk about Chaucer's *persona*, meaning the "I" in his poetry. I have little hesitation in saying that nine-tenths of this talk is misguided and palpably mistaken. It is wrong because it was conceived in and of a world of printed books, and bases its premises and assumptions on conditions which could not obtain in any other. Lip service is paid from time to time to the knowledge that Chaucer wrote for oral delivery, but this primary fact is continually lost sight of or ignored by those who write on the *persona*, and its implications are seldom fully realized.[31]

---

26   "Chaucer: Motive and Mask in the *General Prologue*", *Modern Language Review* 58 (1963): 1–9, at 9.
27   "Chaucer's Point of View as Narrator in the Love Poems", *PMLA* 74 (1959): 511–20, at 520.
28   Ibid., 520.
29   Ibid., 513.
30   "The *Book of the Duchess* Re-opened", *PMLA* 67 (1952): 863–81.
31   *In Search of Chaucer*. Toronto: University of Toronto Press, 1960: 26.

Those implications, Bronson says, are that the "I" in his poetry will be conflated with Geoffrey Chaucer, the real person:

> In view of the conditions confronting Chaucer as poet, what he did not specify as an exceptional requirement his audiences would neither assume nor imagine; and that when he wanted them to attribute words and sentiments to another character, he always made that clear. The schizoid notion of two Chaucers, so named, presented simultaneously, one a puppet, the other the living, speaking poet, with attitudes and intelligences radically different from each other's, could only have arisen in a time when authors would habitually think of themselves as completely separable from their books, and from their audiences, so that when they chose they could make the first personal pronoun stand for anyone they pleased.[32]

In other words, the oral context demands a reconsideration of Donaldson's approach to Chaucer's narrators, because modern literary affectations could have held no currency in a culture in which texts are more often heard than read. The ironic narrators of Jonathan Swift, T. S. Eliot's argument that "honest criticism and sensitive appreciation is directed not upon the poet but upon the poetry",[33] and the fallible narrator of Ford Madox Ford's *The Good Soldier* represent individual historical attitudes towards literary creation and not universal laws of literature.

Nonetheless, many Chaucerians throughout the latter half of the twentieth century continued to read Chaucer's narrator as a literary affectation and an entirely fictional character.[34] In 1965, George Kane warned against using poetry as a source of information about the poet, because this "autobiographical fallacy" denies the distance that must exist between poet and narrator.[35] Narratives of Chaucer's period eas-

---

32 Ibid., 28.
33 "Tradition and the Individual Talent", in *Selected Essays*. New York: Harcourt, 1932: 13–22, at 17.
34 A notable exception is Donald R. Howard, "Chaucer the Man", *PMLA* 80 (1965): 337–43, whose cogent argument suggests that the theories of Donaldson *prove* that Chaucer's human voice permeates the persona and can be seen as a rhetorical device that "can be analyzed by distinguishing between the author and his projected persona" (337).
35 "The Autobiographical Fallacy in Chaucer and Langland Studies", reproduced in George Kane, *Chaucer and Langland*. London: Athlone Press, 1989: 1–14.

ily lead to this fallacy, partly because of "the absence, in fourteenth-century England, of any convention of detached, impersonal narrative. A tale implied a teller; and this was, by implication as well as by his vocal use of the first person, the poet".[36] Yet, Kane insists, we cannot forget that "the dreamers and narrators of Chaucer and Langland are, if I may use jargon, constructs",[37] and the distance between the poet and his construct is, by necessity, absolute.

This approach is distinct in much Chaucerian criticism. Charles Muscatine's enormously influential study insists that readers can maintain a "mildly ironical superiority over him [the narrator]", and that there is a continual "distance between ... the Narrator and the elevated objects of his narration".[38] Thomas J. Garbáty suggests that the narrator is "reasonable", and his position is that of "a man who does not quite understand",[39] and readings of the narrator as the victim of Chaucer's irony are common; thus Elaine Tuttle Hansen argues that the narrator of the *Legend of Good Women* is untrustworthy due to his "undisguised boredom".[40] Chaucer's narrators, it seems, welcome contempt; they are straw men whose flawed position cannot be Chaucer's.

Occasionally, the distance between poet and construct is read not as an opportunity for irony, but as a literary device. Thomas H. Bestul sees the narrator of *Troilus and Criseyde* as an intrusive voice whose emotional interjections are not reflections of Chaucer's own emotions, but attempts "to heighten the emotional response to the subject matter of the story and to raise, by implication, moral questions about the proper response to secular narrative".[41] On the other hand, the narrator's position as the teller of a story has lead many critics to find in him a particular agency. Winthrop Wetherbee argues that Chaucer reduces

36 Ibid., 8.
37 Ibid., 12.
38 *Chaucer and the French Tradition.* Berkeley, Calif.: University of California Press, 1957: 104–5.
39 "The Degradation of Chaucer's 'Geffrey'", *PMLA* 89 (1974): 97–104, at 97–8.
40 "Irony and the Antifeminist Narrator in Chaucer's *Legend of Good Women*", *Journal of English and Germanic Philology* 82 (1983): 11–31, at 29.
41 "Chaucer's *Troilus and Criseyde*: The Passionate Epic and its Narrator", *Chaucer Review* 14 (1980): 366–78, at 366.

his narrator in *Troilus and Criseyde* "to a virtually unconscious collaboration in the discovery of his true poetic vocation".[42] Wetherbee sees in this an imaginative exploration of how much "spiritual enlightenment" is offered by the "olde clerkes", and Chaucer's narrator, as a result, is the one who presents this philosophical exposition.[43] Richard Waswo's study of the same narrator leads him to argue that the text's presentation of "the claims and attitudes of the 'courtly' and 'bourgeois' styles" is not Chaucer's invention, but the narrator's:

> The weaver of this seamless fabric is of course the narrator, who, along with his main original contribution to the story, the character of Pandarus, opens the courtly conventions to realistic criticism and manages at the same time to evoke the higher values that will find both idealism and practicality inadequate, but will only become explicit at the very end of the poem.[44]

Similarly, John Stephens[45] argues for an active fictional narrator in some of Chaucer's lyrics, such as "The Complaint Unto Pity" and "Fortune", and Larry Sklute argues that "Chaucer's persona in the dream visions is a consistent character".[46] J. J. Anderson refines this view to suggest that the narrator "has his own individuality and his own meaning, which are part of the distinctive meaning of the work in which he appears, and which mark him out from the narrators of other poems".[47]

David Lawton was one of the first to develop a sustained criticism of this approach, suggesting instead that the voice of Chaucer's narrator shifts in the text he tells because he is an allegorised abstraction that "partakes in, and is, a discursive event belonging to the

---

42 "'*Per te poeta fui, per te cristiano*': Dante, Statius, and the Narrator of Chaucer's *Troilus*", in *Vernacular Poetics in the Middle Ages*, Lois Ebin (ed.). Kalamazoo, Mich.: Medieval Institute Publications, 1984: 153–76, at 169.
43 Ibid.
44 "The Narrator of Troilus and Criseyde", *ELH* 50 (1983): 1–25, at 2.
45 "The Uses of Personae and the Art of Obliqueness in Some Chaucer Lyrics, Part I", *Chaucer Review* 21 (1987): 360–73.
46 *Virtue of Necessity: Inconclusiveness and Narrative Form in Chaucer's Poetry*. Columbus, Ohio: Ohio State University Press, 1984: 23.
47 "The Narrators in the *Book of the Duchess* and the *Parlement of Foules*", *Chaucer Review* 26 (1992): 219–35, at 219.

work's time – a time other than the author's. This sort of 'I' is therefore a vanishing-point, all but signifying the author's absence".[48] The narrator, Lawton suggests, is not as much a closed, fictional persona as it is a rhetorical mask employed for "local effects", or as an aspect of representation similar to devices such as *amplificatio* and personification.[49] To see this aspect of the narrator, we must see him as an "open" persona – a figure whose purpose is to elicit responses in the audience and to create tonal emphases and complexity that are not self-contradiction, but irresolvable to a singular doctrine or authority."[50]

In recent years, critics have become less satisfied with the narrator-as-fiction approach. Gerald Morgan reminds us that "the theory of the obtuse narrator" is, after all, "no more than a theory",[51] and A. C. Spearing's attack on it is perhaps the most radical. He concedes, rather cynically, that a gap between the tale and its teller is useful, for it "provides a means of rejecting anything that a modern reader finds disagreeable as the responsibility not of Chaucer but of that teller."[52] This use of the fictional-narrator as an exit-clause demands replacement, and Spearing suggests that we should not only do away with the idea of the fictional narrator, but with the idea of narrators altogether. The form of this "narratorless narrative", as Spearing calls it, is a textual encoding of subjectivity through the use of

> linguistic phenomena such as deixis, without the preconceived expectation that these markers will form a unified pattern designating the text as ... 'the product of a particular consciousness', or that the presence of any such pattern will be an index of the writer's success.[53]

The result is a reading of Chaucer, and of medieval literature in general, that eschews the presence of a voice in texts, opting instead for

---

48 *Chaucer's Narrators*. Cambridge: D. S. Brewer, 1985: xiii.
49 Ibid., 6.
50 See also Lawton's "Skelton's Use of *Persona*", *Essays in Criticism* 30 (1980): 9–28.
51 "Moral and Social Identity and the Idea of Pilgrimage in the *General Prologue*", *Chaucer Review* 37 (2003): 285–314, at 288.
52 *Textual Subjectivity*. Oxford: Oxford University Press, 2005: 106.
53 Ibid., 33.

what Spearing calls "subjectless subjectivity". This counter-intuitive notion of narrative insists that, in *Troilus and Criseyde*, "pervasive and flexible *personalizing* does not necessarily imply *impersonation* of a narrator"; the moments of deixis we find, Spearing insists, "have no fixed point of origin".[54] Thus he reads *Troilus and Criseyde* as a written poem "frequently mimetic of oral storytelling", giving credence to the notion that the experience of its first-person voice is unstable and the textual embodiment of subjectivity, instead of a communicative signal from a sender to a receiver.[55] The various personalisation techniques of the poem define a figure "existing both inside and outside 'Thise woful vers, that wepen as I write' (1.7) – a line attributing double agency and double proximity to the verses of the poem and to the 'I' who writes them."[56] As a deictic marker, the first-person pronoun refers but does not represent; it merely encodes a subjective position without itself being an imaginary character – an "ontologically consistent human being", as Spearing puts it.[57]

I am most interested in the function of Chaucer's first-person narrator as a reference to a figure existing both inside and outside the text, for it is from this perspective that the rhetorical power of the narrator as a *topos* becomes most apparent. While I do not hold tenable Spearing's argument for a "subjectless subjectivity" and a voiceless text, partly because Chaucer wrote texts to be read aloud (see below), it is important to retain Spearing's conception of narrative as necessitating a subjective position that tells the story but is not necessarily a consistent fiction. Whether or not it is true that the "subject of narration is not a self",[58] as Spearing insists in no uncertain terms, Chaucer's poetry is unusually self-conscious, even by modern standards. Geffrey in the *House of Fame*, the narrator's emotional engagement (or lack thereof) with the Man in Black's sorrow in the *Book of the*

---

54 Ibid., 94.
55 "A Ricardian 'I': The Narrator of *Troilus and Criseyde*", in *Essays on Ricardian Literature*, A. J. Minnis, Charlotte C. Morse, and Thorlac Turville-Petre (eds.). Oxford: Clarendon Press, 1997: 1–22, at 18. See also *Textual Subjectivity*, 68–100.
56 "A Ricardian 'I'", 18.
57 *Textual Subjectivity*, 52.
58 Ibid., 157.

Duchess, and the deeply self-reflective *Tale of Sir Thopas*, *Tale of Melibee*, and *Retraction* all suggest that Chaucer was not only sometimes concerned with "a conception of the literary text as 'the product of a particular consciousness'",[59] but that he was deeply interested in shaping his audience's perceptions of himself through his texts.

It would be impossible to generalise Chaucer's motivations for doing so, since they differ from poem to poem and, significantly, develop as his own perception of himself as a poet for an English audience evolves. Generalisation is also impossible because each poem has its own purpose, and Chaucer's narratorial personae actively engage in that purpose both to frame the text and to encourage his audience members to find resolution.

Orality

For this study, the context of Chaucer's initial reception is important because it is what he anticipated when producing his texts and their narrators. The experience of hearing a text being read aloud – often referred to as "prelection"[60] – involves a perception of language and the transmission of texts quite different from the assumed model of communication developed in, and for, cultures whose experience of text is mostly private and silent.

Prelection is not restricted in terms of who does the performing; the term refers both to one's performance of one's own work and to one's performance of a text written by someone else. In a rhetorical analysis, however, a distinction needs to be made between these very

---

59 Ibid., 33. The phrase "the product of a particular consciousness" is from Michel Zink, *The Invention of Literary Subjectivity*, David Sices (trans.). Baltimore: Johns Hopkins University Press, 1999.
60 See, for example, Joyce Coleman, *Public Reading and the Reading Public in Late Medieval England and France.* Cambridge: Cambridge University Press, 1996: 155–75 and Dennis Green, "Orality and Reading: The State of Research in Medieval Studies". *Speculum* 65 (1990): 267–80.

different situations. In the pages that follow, I will refer to the action of a writer reading his text aloud to an audience of hearers as "auto-prelection" and will distinguish between this and other forms of prelection. Besides early fifteenth century manuscript illuminations of Chaucer reading aloud to an audience, evidence, admittedly limited, of this practice can be found in the lais of Marie de France, Thomas Chestre's *Sir Launfal*, and Chaucer's *House of Fame*. In each case, the author of the text names himself or herself in the voice of the "narrator", and freely uses the first person singular pronoun in the narration of the tale. The implication of these texts is that of an author speaking directly to an audience in a situation in which they are expected to respond. Auto-prelection implies a certain dynamic between author and audience, whose proximity and communal experience of the text invite a shared mediation of meaning instead of the more unidirectional situation of private reading, in which an individual's immediate responses to a text, however passionate, are distanced from the person of the author. This context, I argue, is particularly relevant for texts such as *Melibee* and *Troilus and Criseyde*, where audience-participation is encouraged by the rhetorical representation of both the author and the audience.

Bronson's description of the context of oral transmission, itself a development of Ruth Crosby's earlier analysis,[61] has since been heavily refined. Joyce Coleman's research on the topic is perhaps the most important. To answer the question of how written texts were read in late medieval England and France, Coleman follows an ethnographic methodology, whereby she draws on historical witnesses to the oral reception of written texts. Among others, John Gower, Thomas Usk, the author of the *Parlement of the Thre Ages*, John Lydgate, and James I of Scotland all refer to the custom of hearing texts being read aloud.[62] On the basis of such references, Coleman concludes that the

---

61 In 1938, Crosby argued that Chaucer's works were intended for oral delivery, and that his aim in writing poetry "was to hold the interest of a fourteenth-century English audience that actually would be listening" and not reading ("Chaucer and the Custom of Oral Delivery", *Speculum* 13 (1938): 413–32, at 432).
62 See ibid., Ch. 7.

prelection of written texts remained popular throughout the fourteenth and fifteenth centuries for the simple reason that people of the era preferred to hear books read, especially if they wanted to be entertained. This perspective allows her to argue against the position maintained by numerous medievalists and theorists of orality, spearheaded by Walter Ong,[63] that with the literate transmission and reception of written texts there is an increase in complexity.[64] For Coleman, the hearing of texts being read in Chaucer's day was not a vestige of an oral culture during a transitory period on an evolutionary march towards literacy, but a social practice that reflected the openness of late medieval society.

The internal evidence for the oral performance of virtually all of Chaucer's works is considerable,[65] and the probability that all these markers of orality are trustworthy seems all the greater when we compare them to contemporary audience addresses and references to public reading. These references have been an embarrassment for some Chaucerians, who have "advanced a number of rather incompatible arguments to explain away ... invocations of aurality [i.e., hearing a text being read aloud]".[66] Some critics refer to Chaucer's "reader" as a matter of course.[67] Edward E. Foster goes so far as to claim that the theory that Chaucer's works were written for an audience of hearers is modern fancy:

---

63 "Oral Residue in Tudor Prose Style", *PMLA* 80 (1965): 145–54; *Orality and Literacy: The Technologizing of the Word*. London: Routledge, 1982; and "Orality, Literacy, and Medieval Textualization", *NLH* 16 (1984): 1–12.
64 Ibid., 1–5.
65 *Public Reading*, 150 and Ch. 6 *passim*.
66 *Public Reading*, 157.
67 See, for example, Dieter Mehl, "Chaucer's Narrator: Troilus and Criseyde and the Canterbury Tales", in *The Cambridge Chaucer Companion*. Piero Boitani and Jill Mann (eds.). Cambridge: Cambridge University Press, 1986: 213–42; Richard Waswo, "The Narrator of Troilus and Criseyde", op. cit., and Arthur W. Bahr, "The Rhetorical Construction of Narrator", op. cit.

there is no direct evidence that Chaucer, or anyone else, ever read the *Tales* or segments of them aloud at court or at any other venue. The evidence for oral presentation is not conclusive.[68]

Yet Foster undermines his argument against prelection before it even begins:

References to Froissart reading *Meliador* to the court of Count Gaston de la Foix do not guarantee that comparable readings occurred at the court of Richard II, though it is not improbable that French customs, like French literature, were mirrored in England.[69]

Other Chaucerians, most notably Derek Brewer, have examined orality as a stylistic feature of Chaucer's works:

In the *Canterbury Tales* the whole scheme is based on the concept of oral storytelling within a group listening to each other. It is conventional because such a situation could only be fictional, and we are more than ever aware of the underlying literacy, even to the extent of being invited to 'turn over the leaf' if we disapprove of a particular story. But by a deep paradox that very invitation is delivered in the style of the poet's speaking voice addressed to us. Though the substance [of the *Canterbury Tales*] is literate the manner is still oral.[70]

Accordingly, the oral markers that pepper Chaucer's works are read as aesthetically motivated. Such a reading, by necessity, ignores the many references to aurality that we find in other contemporaneous texts. Brewer also polarises the oral world and the literate into separate realms of communication; Chaucer presents literature in the oral style in an attempt to blend "the new world of literate thought into the old but always current world of personal direct speech and relationship".[71] This argument fits Ong's evolutionary model, which is the basis for Brewer's study.

---

68   "Has Anyone Here Read *Melibee?*", *Chaucer Review* 34 (2000): 398–409, at 406.
69   Ibid.
70   "Chaucer's Poetic Style", in *The Cambridge Chaucer Companion*, Piero Boitani and Jill Mann (eds.). Cambridge: Cambridge University Press, 1986: 85–119.
71   Ibid., 227.

This reading of the Chaucerian oral style as a literary affectation and a stylistic posturing implies that Chaucer's non-literary texts, particularly his prose treatises, should contain no affectations of orality whatsoever. Edward E. Foster did not express an uncommon sentiment when he wrote that the *Tale of Melibee* is "less suited for oral reading than any other [tale in the *Canterbury Tales*] except the *Parson's Tale*".[72] We today, upon approaching the *Parson's Tale* and the *Treatise on the Astrolabe*, may find it difficult to imagine an audience who would hear such texts being read aloud. Yet Chaucer does. Even in the *Treatise*, a long prose work and technical textbook, he envisions an audience who will hear the text be read when he addresses "every discret persone that redith or herith this litel tretys" (41–50).[73] If we were to extend the arguments of Derek Brewer and Edward E. Foster to the *Treatise*, this audience address would become a stylistic affectation of orality. Yet what would this be doing in a treatise written to help foster Lewis Chaucer's "abilite to lerne sciences touching nombres and proporciouns" (1)? Was Chaucer conjuring for his son the fantasy of hearing the *Treatise* being read to him? It is more likely that this is not an affectation, but a straightforward address to an audience who will receive the written text in one or two modes of textual reception, as referred to in Caxton's editions of a century later. And if a prose work as technical as the *Treatise* was written for an audience of hearers as well as readers, it is reasonable to assume that any of Chaucer's other works could equally have been written for oral performance, whether by the author or another person.

In Chaucer's *Retraction*, quite possibly the last of his writings, he again addresses an audience of hearers and readers:

> Now preye I to hem alle that herkne this litel tretys or rede, that if ther be any thyng in it that liketh hem, that therof they thank our Lord Jhesu Crist, of whom procedeth al wit and al goodnesse. (X.1081)

The manuscript history of the *Retraction* suggests that the "litel tretys" Chaucer here refers to is in fact the *Parson's Tale*. Mícaél F. Vaughan

---

72 "Has Anyone Here Read *Melibee*?", 407.
73 All quotations of Chaucer are from the *Riverside Chaucer*, 3rd edn, Larry D. Benson (ed.). Boston: Houghton Mifflin, 1987.

observes that the two were kept together in the earliest manuscripts, while Charles Owen, Jr. suggests that the *Parson's Tale* is an independent treatise on patience, for which the *Retraction* is a fitting conclusion.[74] Other scholars have also seen a strong link between the two; Lee Patterson,[75] Douglas Wurtele,[76] and Kieran Kealy[77] see the *Parson's Tale* as a preparatory step to Chaucer's ultimate renunciation of his fictive works. Douglas Wurtele even argues that lines 1081–4 and 1090(b)–2 were originally part of the *Parson's Tale* as its epilogue, a theory still held by some Chaucerians.[78] Thus it is likely that the phrase "litel tretys" here refers to the *Parson's Tale* – an increasingly likely possibility in light of Chaucer's other uses of the word to refer to long expository works in prose.

It also seems that Chaucer expected his readers to be the minority. When addressing his audience, he refers to those who "herkne this litel tretys *or rede*"; his reference to readers appears to be an afterthought, while the hearers of the written text are given a more syntactically natural position. Also noteworthy is the absence of the preposition "of" or "to" after the verb "hearken". This is common in Chaucer's usage of the verb, which more often carries a prepositionless object than not, unlike the modern equivalent "listen".[79] This

---

74 Míceál F. Vaughan, "Creating Comfortable Boundaries: Scribes, Editors, and the Invention of the Parson's Tale", in *Rewriting Chaucer: Culture, Authority, and the Idea of the Authentic Text, 1400–1602*; Thomas A. Prendergast and Barbara Kline (eds.). Columbus: Ohio State University Press, 1999: 45–90; and Charles A. Owen Jr., "What the Manuscripts Tell Us about the Parson's Tale", *Medium Ævum* 63 (1994): 239–49.
75 "The *Parson's Tale* and the Quitting of the *Canterbury Tales*", *Traditio* 34 (1978): 331–80.
76 "The Penitence of Geoffrey Chaucer", *Viator* 11 (1980): 335–61.
77 "Voices of the Tabard: The Last Tales of the Canterbury Tales", in *From Arabye to Engelond: Medieval Studies in Honour of Mahmoud Manzalaoui on His 75th Birthday*. A. E. Christa Canitz and Gernot R. Wieland (eds.). Ottawa: University of Ottawa Press, 1999: 113–29.
78 Matthew C. Wolfe, "Placing Chaucer's *Retraction* for a Reception of Closure", *Chaucer Review* 33 (1999): 427–31.
79 To restrict myself to the *Canterbury Tales*, cf. *GP* 788, 855, *KtT* 1526, 2532, 2674, *MT* 3136, *MLT* 425, 1174, *WbT* 14, *FrT* 1656, *ClT* 1176, *MeT* 1310, *FlT* 1496, *PT* 521, *StT* 893, *NPT* 3201, 3210, 3402, *SnT* 261, *CyT* 691, 927, 1006,

might suggest that listening to texts being read aloud was so common that the use of a preposition in the verb phrase might have seemed pleonastic. Today, listening to a text is so unusual that a preposition is needed to reinforce the connection between "listening" and "text".

If Chaucer not only wrote for hearers, but for auto-prelection, then Chaucer's audience addresses imply a more intimate and reciprocal relationship between author and audience and give the text a more social dynamic than, say, a novel written to be read alone by individuals. Thus Joyce Coleman suggests that "medieval readers chose to share their experience of literature because they valued shared experience".[80] I hope to show that Chaucer's emphasis on his own private reading, through the figure of his narrator, is at odds with the valued shared experience of public reading that was so natural for his contemporary, intended audience. If, as Coleman suggests, "a book read aloud came alive not only with the performer's voice but with the listeners' reactions and responses, with their concentration, their tears and applause, their philosophical or political debates, and their demands that the page be turned",[81] then any representation of reading that contrasted with this shared, communal and social experience would give hearers pause. Further, the text's textual representation of the author's voice becomes a part of its significance, as it allows the author to become part of the community of the text in each performance.

Chaucer and the Rhetoric of Self-Representation

Donaldson warns that

> Verisimilitude in a work of fiction is not without its attendant dangers, the chief of which is that the responses it stimulates in the reader may be those ap-

---

PrT 363, 373, 648, 1003, 1004, and *R* 1082. Exceptions to this are *MeT* 1699, *ShT* 23, *PrT* 498, where Chaucer used the preposition "of", in the case of the *Merchant's Tale*, or "to", as in the case of the *Shipman's Tale* and the *Parson's Tale*.
80 *Public Reading*, 221.
81 Ibid.

propriate not so much to an imaginative production as to an historical one or to a piece of reporting.[82]

This book is an attempt to recover what sort of responses the verisimilitude of Chaucer's narrator might have invited in his contemporary audience – those men and women of his era for whom he was ultimately writing, not the general "reader" Donaldson posits. Such a study might, at first glance, seem an unduly naive conflation of narrator and author – the fallacy that Donaldson and his followers insist must be avoided. But such an emphasis does not read Chaucer's narrator as Chaucer any more than it reads him as a fiction, since it focuses on the narrator as a collection of textually encoded rhetorical gestures whose purpose is to persuade.

I am largely motivated to read in this way by Chaucer's near-contemporary reception. So many fifteenth century readers and admirers of Chaucer praised his rhetorical skill over all else. Partly this can be seen as a historical inevitability; little distinction was made between rhetoric and poetry in fourteenth and fifteenth century England, and our own negative attitudes towards rhetoric, as a mask of truth or a sophisticated means of cynical self-service, are not met with similar opprobrium in the generations immediately following Chaucer. E. F. Dyck notes that "distinctions between poetry and rhetoric conceal as much as they reveal. One such distinction, that poetry is imitation and rhetoric is persuasion, conceals the fact that, in addition to imitating, literature persuades."[83] The author of the "Book of Curtesye" was keenly aware of literature's persuasiveness when he noted how Chaucer knew "how to plese in euery audyence".

In what follows I hope to show how Chaucer attempted to please his audience. My purpose is to embark upon a full-length study of Chaucer's narrator as an agent of persuasion – a mask that exists to influence audiences. I argue that what lies between the construct and the real person is a rhetorical space, potentially manipulated by the poet to influence his audience's perception of the writer both as an

---

82   "Chaucer the Pilgrim", 928.
83   "Ethos, Pathos, and Logos in *Troilus and Criseyde*", *Chaucer Review* 20 (1986): 169–81, at 169.

author and as a member of his society. To some extent, this is an extension of the approaches developed by E. T. Donaldson and George Kane, but in the pages that follow I remain committed to Bertrand Bronson counterarguments. The oral context of Chaucer's reception, and the circumstance of auto-prelection that I presume he wrote for, were central to the imaginative construction of his persona as a representation of his voice. But generalisations about Chaucer's narrator, so often attempted in the past, cannot be made because the individual strategies and contexts of each text demand a shift in this narrative voice, much as a question or an exclamation demands a shift in inflection. Hopefully, a rhetorical emphasis will move the debate beyond the reductive dichotomy of whether the narrator is or is not a fiction by examining how Chaucer encourages us to read the narrator as the author, forgetting that he is really an aspect of the author's self-representation, ever changing to suit Chaucer's rhetorical needs. The following chapters are an attempt to understand the rhetorical impact of these shifts and the possible motivations behind them.

Chapter 2
The Consoler: *Book of the Duchess*

The *Book of the Duchess*, Its Date and Audience

Sometimes a poem cannot be understood without an intimate knowledge of the personal lives it involves. *Book of the Duchess* is such a poem; Chaucer's motives in writing this work and its effects on his contemporary audience were intricately linked to a network of intersecting private and public relationships between Chaucer and John of Gaunt that developed after the death of the nobleman's first wife, Blanche, duchess of Lancaster. For this reason, dating the poem is essential to understanding it. We have known that Blanche died on 12 September 1368 since J. J. N. Palmer published a letter written in late 1368 from Louis de Mâle, count of Flanders to Queen Philippa touching upon the duchess's death, and thus the poem could not have been written before that date.[1]

To move from this *terminus a quo* to a *terminus ad quem* requires much interpretation of circumstantial evidence, and thus allows room for debate and disagreement. John of Gaunt's order of an alabaster tomb for Blanche for the sixth anniversary memorial of her death in 1374[2] has invited some to argue that Chaucer wrote the poem for a performance coinciding with, or as a part of, that ceremony.[3] Others hold 1371 or 1372 as the last possible year of composition.

---

[1] J. J. N. Palmer, "The Historical Context of the *Book of the Duchess:* A Revision", *Chaucer Review* 8 (1974): 253–61.

[2] N. B. Lewis, "The Anniversary Service for Blanche, Duchess of Lancaster, 12th September 1374", *Bulletin of the John Rylands Library* 21 (1937): 3–19.

[3] For one of the most influential of these datings, see D. W. Robertson, "The Historical Setting of Chaucer's *Book of the Duchess*", in *Medieval Studies in Honor of Urban Tigner Holmes*, John Mahoney and Jon Esten Keller (eds.). Chapel Hill, NC, 1966: 169–95.

Palmer believes the poem could not have been written after Gaunt's marriage to Costanza, princess of Castile, in 1371, when it would have been seen as a satirical portrait of Gaunt as an "Inconstant Lover".[4] Howard Schless disagrees, and points out that although we might find the poem inappropriate after Gaunt's remarriage, such a view is "a projection of our own morality" onto Chaucer's day, when political marriages were the norm amongst the aristocracy.[5] The fact that Louis de Mâle's letter was written a scant three and a half months after the death of Blanche to suggest a "mariage de mon trescher cousin le duc de Lancastre, votre filz, et de ma fille", "a marriage between my beloved cousin the Duke of Lancaster, your son, and my daughter"[6] underlines the fact that marriage and love were not necessarily linked for John of Gaunt's social class.

Schless suggests that we should date the poem to after "the end of 1371, or perhaps 1372", after John of Gaunt had received Edward III's permission to assume the title of King of Castile and Leon, based upon line 1314: "With that me thoghte that this kyng",[7] although Edward I. Condren notes that this "king" is in fact Octavian, whose hart-hunt, narrated earlier in the poem, is the subject of the preceding three lines:

> And with that word ryght anoon
> They gan to strake forth; al was doon,
> For that tyme, the hert-huntyng. (1311–13)[8]

That this king is not in fact Gaunt opens up a pre-1372 dating, and the possibility that the poem was written shortly after Blanche's death, perhaps at the request of Queen Philippa. Another clue that confirms such a date is the reference to Richmond in line 1319 ("ryche hil"), of which Gaunt was an earl until 20 July 1372, when Edward III trans-

---

4   Palmer, "The Historical Context", 259–60.
5   Howard Schless, "A Dating for the *Book of the Duchess:* Line 1314", *Chaucer Review* 19 (1985): 272–6.
6   Reproduced in Palmer, "The Historical Context", 253.
7   Schless, "Dating", 274.
8   Possibly significant is the fact that reference is made to Lancaster and Richmond, but not to Castile. See "The Historical Context of the Book of the Duchess: A New Hypothesis", *Chaucer Review* 5 (1970): 195–212.

ferred the earldom to John de Montfort to secure his loyalty to England in the struggle because he, as Sydney Armitage-Smith notes, "was wavering between England and France".[9] This was not a disgraceful loss; Gaunt had quickly succumbed to Edward III's will for the good of the country, and he was amply rewarded with

> The castle of Pevensey, the castle, Honor, and manor of the High Peak, together with manors, franchises, and advowsons in half a dozen counties, Nottingham, Huntingdon, Cambridge, Norfolk, Suffolk and Sussex.[10]

Although Gaunt lost Richmond to Montfort, he may still have been identified with Richmond for quite some time, and since he sacrificed his claim to Richmond to strengthen England's position against France during the war, the lands could have been perceived after 1372 as a symbol of Gaunt's grace and patriotism. Since he was an unpopular figure throughout his life,[11] this reference to Richmond could have been additional flattery if the poem was written after his sacrifice. However, a post-1372 dating must consider the repercussions an identification of Gaunt with Richmond would entail; as flattering as it would be to Gaunt, it might have been annoying, insulting, or even threatening to the new Earl of Richmond and possibly Edward III himself. For this reason, I am in agreement with Palmer that the poem was most likely written and performed before July 1372. A pre-1372 dating has held much sway in recent years.[12]

---

9   *John of Gaunt*. London: Constable and Company, 1904: 202.
10 Ibid., 202–3.
11 For an account of Gaunt's reputation, see ibid., 121–36.
12 Beryl Rowland, "Chaucer's Duchess and Chess", *Florilegium* 16 (1999): 41–60, at 42 and Kathryn L. Lynch, *Chaucer's Philosophical Visions* Cambridge: D. S. Brewer, 2000: 31. Robert A. Watson confidently dates the poem to 1369 ("Dialogue and Invention in the *Book of the Duchess*", *Modern Philology* 98 (2001): 543–76, at 545). Jenny Adams argues that the poem must have been written before 1372, although without explanation ("Pawn Takes Knight's Queen: Playing with Chess in the *Book of the Duchess*", *Chaucer Review* 34 (1999): 125–38, at 135). A.J. Minnis, *Oxford Guides to Chaucer: The Shorter Poems.* Oxford: Oxford University Press, 1995: 79–80 notes in parentheses that the reference to Richmond confirms that the poem was written before Gaunt lost that earldom. Three exceptions are Phillipa Hardman, who dates the poem

At the time of Blanche's death, Chaucer was probably not in the country. On 17 July 1368 he was granted a licence to pass at Dover with "vint soldz por ses despenses", "twenty shillings for personal expenses",[13] and appears next in the records on 20 October 1368, when Edward III ordered a mandate to pay Chaucer his annuity in arrears.[14] At the same time, John of Gaunt was in England, quite probably, as Donald R. Howard suggests, at Blanche's bedside when she died.[15] Chaucer would most likely have heard of the duchess's death over a month after the fact, when the initial wave of Gaunt's and England's grief had begun to ebb.

Surviving records give the impression that Chaucer's connections to Gaunt at this time were minimal. Possibly, Chaucer first met Gaunt when he was a page in the household of Elizabeth, countess of Ulster, where he served from 1357 to 1359,[16] but his minor position as one of the many pages in the Ulster household would not have allowed for anything more than a formal meeting. The records do not provide a tangible link between the two by the time of the duchess's death, and although it is possible that they gained some familiarity in the years 1361–5, for which we have no records, it is more likely that

to 1374, Nicole Lassahn, who suggests that the poem "could have been written as late as after 1374", and William A. Quinn, who bases a date "closer to 1374 than 1368" upon a reading of the poem as an attempt to "put the Duke's grief to rest, not just to eulogize the memory of the dead Duchess": Hardman, "The *Book of the Duchess* as a Memorial Monument", *Chaucer Review* 28 (1994): 205–15; Lassahn, "Literary Representations of History in Fourteenth Century England: Shared Technique and Divergent Practice in Chaucer and Langland", *Essays in Medieval Studies* 17 (2000): 49–58, at 51–2: and Quinn, "Medieval Dream Visions: Chaucer's *Book of the Duchess*", in *Readings in Medieval Texts: Interpreting Old and Middle English Literature*, David Johnson and Elaine Treharne (eds.). Oxford: Oxford University Press, 2005: 323–36. Larry D. Benson and Colin Wilcockson date the poem to before 1372 – see *Riverside Chaucer*, xxix and 329, respectively.

13   Reproduced in Martin M. Crow and Clair C. Olson, *Chaucer Life-Records* Oxford: Clarendon Press, 1966: 29.
14   Reproduced in ibid., 128.
15   Donald R. Howard, *Chaucer: His Life, His Works, His World.* New York, NY: Ballentine Books, 1987: 122.
16   *Life-Records*, 13–18.

the two did not interact too greatly, given Chaucer's low social status in comparison to Gaunt, then one of the most powerful aristocrats in England.

A personal link between the two would not emerge until 30 August 1372, when the duke began to give annuities to the poet's wife, Philippa Chaucer.[17] Gaunt would not award Chaucer an annuity until nearly two years later,[18] which, as Paul Strohm has noted, did not compromise or contradict his loyalty to the king's court.[19] Although Chaucer's sister-in-law, Katherine Swynford, was attached to Blanche's court until the duchess's death, this does not suggest that John of Gaunt had more than a passing familiarity with Katherine, let alone any connection to her sister or brother-in-law, until she had begun her duties as the governess of Gaunt's and Blanche's children upon the death of their mother.[20] It was probably around this time that the two began having a romantic relationship. Sydney Armitage-Smith maintains that the affair between Gaunt and Katherine probably began in 1371 or 1372, observing that John Beaufort, their first child, was born in 1373.[21] Thus the first opportunity for meaningful contact between

---

17 The first record of an annuity paid to Philippa Chaucer by John of Gaunt is from 30 August 1372, reproduced in *Life-Records*, 85–6.
18 The grant for the annuity is reproduced in *Life-Records*, 271.
19 *Social Chaucer*. Cambridge, Mass.: Harvard University Press, 1989: 34–6.
20 *John of Gaunt*, 390–1.
21 Ibid., 389 and 462–3. Armitage-Smith quotes the Monk of Evesham, who writes that the relationship began during Gaunt's marriage to Constance, and Froissart, who tells us that the relationship began around the time of the death of Katherine's first husband, Hugh Swynford, in 1372. The year of John Beaufort's birth is not given in surviving records. Anthony Goodman accepts Armitage-Smith's dating in his biography, *John of Gaunt: The Exercise of Princely Power in Fourteenth-Century Europe*. London: Longman, 1992: 365. G. L. Harriss suggests that he was born in 1372 "before she [Katherine] was widowed" (see Harriss, *Cardinal Beaufort: A Study of Lancastrian Ascendancy and Decline*. Oxford: Clarendon Press, 1988); in his 2004 entry for the *Oxford Dictionary of National Biography*, Harriss suggests c.1371 for Beaufort's birth. Any of these dates suggests that the liaison began at some point in 1371. Due to length restrictions and a paucity of documents, I shall not explore whether the liaison began before or after Hugh Swynford's death nor how this might have further complicated public perceptions of Gaunt's relationships with Katherine and Blanche.

Gaunt and Chaucer would have been around this time and would have been the result of a private, intimate, and non-political relationship.

If the *Book of the Duchess* was written after the affair between Gaunt and Swynford began, its social function as a propaganda poem must be considered. Since Swynford had worked in Blanche's household, it would be surprising if some did not consider whether Gaunt had begun his affair before Blanche's death, and if he did truly love his first wife; Chaucer's poem quells such doubts by depicting Gaunt's intense emotional bereavement. Although the poem has often been seen as a plea for patronage and a literary exploration of the relationship between nobleman and poets (see below), Chaucer may have written the poem to defend his sister-in-law's name as much as to vie for Gaunt's patronage.

The poem's social functions and implicit context do not contradict its inherent consolation, which makes it one of the most moving and beautiful of Chaucer's works. Chaucer is careful to avoid referring to the complex social situation surrounding Gaunt. Ostensibly, the poem attempts to comfort a bereaved man who has lost a woman he passionately loved. This is also the context that best suits many passages, such as the Man in Black's final declaration that his lady is dead:

> "She ys ded!" "Nay!" "Yis, be my troughe!"
> "Is that youre los? Be God, hyt ys routhe!"
> And with that word ryght anoon
> They [the hart-hunters] gan to strake forth; al was doon,
> For that tyme, the hert-huntyng. (1309–13)

Blanche is dead, and so the hunt for the hart/heart has ended, and all will go home in a lamenting, solemn mood. Then, after Chaucer has revealed the Man in Black's identity, he describes how the lady's death was marked by the ringing of church bells:

> Ryght thus me mette, as I yow telle,
> That in the castell ther was a belle,
> As hyt hadde smyten houres twelve. (1321–3)

Now that he has told the narrator that she is dead, the bells ring, as bells did during a funeral mass. The number twelve also recalls the narrator's initial attempt to console the Man in Black's loss:

> "Ne say noght soo, for trewely,
> Thogh ye had lost the ferses twelve,
> And ye for sorwe mordred yourselve,
> Ye sholde be dampned in this cas." (722–5)

The depth of the Man in Black's sorrow, which has almost lead him to suicide, stresses one of the themes of the poem: Blanche was worth at least twelve queens, and we are to pity Gaunt for his immeasurable loss.

However, some have seen this poem as a literary experiment more theoretical and impersonal in scope and significance. Whereas earlier scholarship accepted that the poem was most likely written for John of Gaunt, either under his patronage or as a plea for it, recent attention has focused upon the heterogeneity of Chaucer's mixed audience, which included readers closer to Chaucer's own social class. Paul Strohm notes that, "Although the composition of this audience cannot securely be known, the confidence with which Chaucer approaches it would argue for relatively greater social equality than that existing between Chaucer and John of Gaunt".[22] Previously held notions of Chaucer as a court poet have invited an antithetical approach to the poem's audience, which ever increasingly excludes John of Gaunt. This false dilemma – was the poem written for Gaunt or for Chaucer's social equals – has assumed that the poem could not have been written for both, and it does not provide a satisfactory account of how Gaunt relates to this very intimate poem about his bereavement for his first wife. Even if the poem were written for just about everyone else but Gaunt, as Strohm implies and more recent scholars have suggested, it strains credulity to imagine that Chaucer would carry on writing his first lengthy narrative on a highly contemporary topic involving the most powerful man in England without expecting the poem to catch its subject's attention at some point.

---

22   Paul Strohm, *Social Chaucer*, 55.

If we maintain that *Book of the Duchess* was written at least partially for John of Gaunt, Chaucer's anticipation of the nobleman's reaction is a part of the fabric of the poem. Gaunt publicly mourned Blanche for the rest of his life, even after marrying Katherine Swynford in January 1396, over twenty years after their relationship had begun,[23] so we can expect *Book of the Duchess* to have elicited thoughts of Gaunt's feelings toward Blanche while expressing, or creating, an emotional bond between the nobleman and poet regardless of when it was written.

Yet the poem is increasingly read as belonging to a literary sphere outside the pragmatic concerns of everyday life. Nicole Lassahn's study of the poem as a "*literary* discussion: a reworking of the ways in which this representation [of the poet-patron relationship] has been used before" is a typical example.[24] Such a reading assumes a literary self-consciousness in Chaucer, which is by no means incompatible with the self-consciousness we find in his other works or in the literary traditions that inspired him, particularly in Machaut's poetry and Jean de Meun's continuation of *Le Roman de la rose*. A literary theme would have been most relevant to a circle of civil servants and administrators, all of whom were professional writers and scribes, and this is the audience that Lassahn assumes for the poem, arguing that "the idea of Chaucer as a poet at court, with royal patrons, may be as much a function of his reception in the fifteenth century, and his own poetics, as it is a reflection of his actual status".[25] The concerns of this

---

23   In his testament, dated 3 February 1398, Gaunt asked to be buried next to Blanche, and he was summarily buried there in 1399. The testament is reproduced in Armitage-Smith, *John of Gaunt*, 420. However, one must consider the protestations made by Derek Pearsall (*The Life of Geoffrey Chaucer*. Oxford: Blackwell, 1992: 89–91), who notes that it was conventional to be buried beside one's first wife, and thus we cannot take Gaunt's will to signify any emotional connection between the two.

24   "Literary Representations", 52, italics retained.

25   Ibid., 50. Lassahn suggests that the fifteenth-century aristocratic audience Seth Lerer observes (*Chaucer and His Readers*. Princeton, NJ: Princeton University Press, 1993: Chs. 1 and 4) need not represent Chaucer's contemporary audience at the end of the fourteenth century. She also suggests that "Gaunt was not Chaucer's patron, and hence not his primary audience, if he was part of his audience at all" (ibid., 53 n.12).

literate "middle-class" audience gravitated largely towards issues of history, politics, and their own position within both. So, Lassahn argues, the issue of love lost

> is not the *setting* for the events and the plot (as it would be in a romance novel involving pirates, for example); rather the subject matter of the works, their plot, is somehow history itself. History itself is what is represented, just as it is in the academic prose narrative created by the historian.[26]

This reading puts Chaucer in a position much like Lassahn's own and that of the modern critic, and turns his poetry into a theoretical discussion instead of a work of literature fixed within a historical time and place. Such decontextualisation allows for an understanding of the *Book of the Duchess* as a "wholly theoretical" work – that is to say, as a literary experiment.[27]

We cannot forget that Lassahn, as a professional academic, was writing in 2000 for an audience entrenched in post-Barthesian approaches to literature, and that her interpretation might reflect her social milieu more than that of the author she is discussing. Evidence contemporary with Chaucer for Lassahn's thesis is not readily available. To believe that his primary audience was *exclusively* this administrative class is to assume that fifteenth century writers such as Thomas Hoccleve typify his contemporary, intended audience, even though there is no evidence to confirm this. Only one of Chaucer's short poems is directly addressed to contemporary figures who were more or less part of his social class (if not slightly beneath him): the "Wordes unto Adam, His Owne Scriveyn", which Linne Mooney has recently shown to be written for the scribe Adam Pinkhurst.[28] It should be mentioned that Pinkhurst's handiwork, the Ellesmere and Hengwrt manuscripts, were disseminated through the upper gentry and noble classes as were most early fifteenth century manuscripts of Chaucer. Further intersections between both classes, especially when

---

26 Ibid., 50.
27 Ibid., 58.
28 "Chaucer's Scribe", *Speculum* 81 (2006): 97–138.

it comes to the buying and selling of manuscripts, are abundant in this era.[29]

We must also take into account the poems to Bukton and Scogan, which address men wealthier and more powerful than Chaucer in a playful, intimate tone. Chaucer also addressed men at the highest level of the social hierarchy: "Lak of Stedfastnesse" was written for Richard II and "The Complaint of Chaucer to His Purse" is addressed to Henry IV. If we were to extend Lassahn's paradigm of theoretical literary construction, we would have to accept that these were not written for their addressed audiences at all, but literary affectations with only a theoretical engagement. Such an argument would also suggest a similar motivation behind the *Wordes unto Adam*, leaving us with no means by which to reconstruct the intended audience of any of Chaucer's works. Such a relativistic argument is not as helpful as a more historical reading, even if such a reading may appear to some a naive acceptance of the clues these poems provide. Not only more pragmatic, but, I think, truer is a reading that assumes *Book of the Duchess* is as Chaucer presents it: an elegy (however problematic) about Blanche written for John of Gaunt.

The poem invites such an interpretation. Hints at Blanche's and Gaunt's identities are easy to spot. The queen whom the Black Knight mourns is called "White" (l.948), an obvious pun on Blanche's name,

---

29 To name a few case studies and references to manuscript exchange between these classes: Kathleen L. Scott, "A Mid Fifteenth-Century English Illuminating Shop and its Customers", *Journal of the Warburg and Courtauld Institutes* 31 (1968): 170–96; J. J. G. Alexander, "Painting and Manuscript Illumination for Royal Patrons in the Later Middle Ages", in *English Court Culture in the Later Middle Ages*, V. J. Scattergood and J. W. Sherborne (eds.). London: Duckworth, 1983: 141–62; Carol M. Meale, "The Compiler At Work: John Colyns and BL MS Harley 2252", in *Manuscripts and Readers in Fifteenth-Century England*, Derek Pearsall (ed.). Cambridge: D. S. Brewer, 1983: 82–103; Carol M. Meale and Julia Boffey, "Gentlewomen's Reading", in *Cambridge History of the Book in Britain: Volume III 1400–1557*, Lotte Hellinga and J. B. Trapp (eds.). Cambridge: Cambridge University Press, 1999: 526–40; and Carol M. Meale, "The Politics of Book Ownership: The Hopton Family and Bodleian Library, Digby MS 185", in *Prestige, Authority and Power in Late Medieval Manuscripts and Texts*, Felicity Riddy (ed.). Woodbridge: Boydell, 2000: 82–103.

and less than oblique references to John of Gaunt march forth at the end of the poem:

> With that me thoghte that this kyng
> Gan homwarde for to ryde
> Unto a place, was there besyde,
> Which was from us but a lyte –
> A long castel with walles white,
> Be Seynt Johan, on a ryche hil,
> As me mette; but thus hyt fil. (1314–20)

Within six lines Chaucer makes references to John of Gaunt's Castilian title (l.1314), his Lancastrian title (the "long castel" of l.1318), Gaunt's name-saint (St Johan, l.1319), and Richmond ("ryche hil", l.1319), discussed above. In this Chaucer follows the conventions of the French poems that preceded and influenced him, which identify the author and intended audience in anagrams at their beginnings and ends. Chaucer is here more direct in making it clear that his poem is about and for a particular person than were the French poets, whose anagrams are often opaque.

The centrality of Chaucer's and Gaunt's relationship to the poem has prompted some scholars, most notably Edward I. Condren,[30] to argue that it is a plea for Gaunt's patronage. At the very least, it would be natural to assume that some sort of relationship, however minor, was well in place by the time the poem was written. If Gaunt had not been a patron, we might believe that he must still have been at least an important figure in Chaucer's life. However, historical records tell us that a public relationship between the two only began in 1374; even then, it was tenuous. At the same time, Chaucer's connections with the monarchy remained strong throughout his lifetime.[31] During 1368–74 and 1389–91 he was a salaried servant of the king's court; afterwards he was a king's esquire and, at least in name, a knight.[32]

---

30 In "The Historical Context of the Book of the Duchess" and "Of Deaths and Duchesses and Scholars Coughing in Ink", *Chaucer Review* 10 (1975): 87–95.
31 Strohm, *Social Chaucer*, 24–46.
32 In the records for 1386, Chaucer is described as a knight ("miles comitatus") of Kent (*Life-Records*, 367). However, he was probably never officially given the title, since it was common to refer to Members of Parliament as knights

From 1368 onwards, Chaucer was dependent upon the king for his income and his social position. This means that, in the years 1368–74, he would have appeared to John of Gaunt and his household as an outsider whose true public place was in the court of Edward III.

I do not mean to politicise the reception of Chaucer and the *Book of the Duchess*. At this point in time, Chaucer was politically unimportant. As a young valet/esquire of Edward III's court, he was simply not a player in politics.[33] What would have been more at the forefront in John of Gaunt's and Chaucer's minds would have been their closer personal relationship.

We know that Chaucer's wife, Philippa, was a member of the Lancastrian household from at least 30 August 1372, and quite possibly before. If Gaunt heard or read the *Book of the Duchess* after this date, then he would have seen Chaucer as an extension of his household through marital ties. If this was the case, the loss of a spouse would have been more than appropriate for Chaucer to write about, because the poem would have been founded upon this already established domestic relationship and not a public or political relationship. However, the reference to Richmond strongly suggests a pre-1372 dating, at some point shortly before or after the relationship between Gaunt and Swynford began. This is, of course, a significant element of the poem's context. If Philippa Chaucer was not a member of Gaunt's household[34] and if Gaunt had not yet begun his relationship with Swynford when Chaucer wrote the *Book of the Duchess*, then the relationship between the two men would have been effectively non-

---

whether they had been dubbed so or not (see *Life-Records*, 366), and records postdating this appointment do not refer to him as a knight. No records exist to suggest a ceremony ever took place.

33   Gerald Morgan believed this to be true throughout Chaucer's life: "On the evidence of his poetry Chaucer is an urbane and reflective man able to pursue a successful diplomatic as well as poetic career at court and in the outward ambience of courts. The political convulsions of the reigns of Edward III, Richard II, and (at the very end of his life) Henry IV, the son of Blanche and John of Gaunt, seem to have left him largely untouched" ("Moral and Social Identity and the Idea of Pilgrimage in the General Prologue", *Chaucer Review* 37 (2003): 285–314, at 286).

34   Our first record of Philippa Chaucer as a member of Gaunt's household comes from 30 August 1372, reproduced in *Life-Records*, 85–7.

existent. It is within this context that the poem becomes an act of mediating the poet's relationship to Gaunt without the foundation of a pre-existing association. The poem's politeness and deferential rhetoric would be consistent with such a context, but it is equally possible that the poem was written after the affair began – perhaps in 1371 or 1372 – and that Chaucer put this deferential rhetoric in place to give Gaunt the impression that he is acutely aware of his lower social status.

The inherent awkwardness of Chaucer's social position pales in comparison to the difficult task that the *Book of the Duchess* presented: consoling a man faced with the sudden loss of his wife. Arthur W. Bahr argues that Chaucer was "[f]aced with the task of comforting her [Blanche's] grieving husband, yet unable to assume the appearance of superior emotional wisdom that would allow him to do so directly".[35] The vast obstacles which Chaucer faced as he put pen to paper came from every direction of life; within this context, the self-deprecating narrator becomes a multi-faceted rhetorical trope that confirms Chaucer's lower social status, admits his inability to console Gaunt, and dignifies the nobleman's feelings of pain and loss.

The Rhetorical Construction of the Narrator

Although it is about Gaunt and Blanche, the main character of the *Book of the Duchess* is the narrator. The poem begins and ends with a focus on him, and follows his transformation from a distressed and ailing insomniac to a daunted, confused dreamer to, finally, a lonely writer. It is thus no surprise that the poem begins with the first person singular pronoun and an expression of individual suffering:

> I have gret wonder, be this lyght,
> How that I lyve, for day ne nyght

---

[35] Arthur W. Bahr, "The Rhetorical Construction of Narrator and Narrative in Chaucer's the *Book of the Duchess*", *Chaucer Review* 35 (2000): 43–59, at 44.

> I may nat slepe wel nygh noght;
> I have so many an ydel thought
> Purely for defaute of slep
> That, by my trouthe, I take no kep
> Of nothing, how hyt cometh or gooth,
> Ne me nys nothyng leef nor looth. (1–8)

From this passage to line 61, the focus of the poem is on the narrator and his ambiguous sickness. At the same time, as Bahr observes, these lines "are noteworthy for how little they tell us, and how little closure, semantic or otherwise, they provide us".[36] Although the emphasis is clearly on the narrator, he is described vaguely and unsatisfactorily, inviting curiosity without appearing grandiose or self-centered.

Because of its vagueness, the narrator's illness has been often debated. Many Chaucerians have seen it as lovesickness, and research by Mary Wack supports this interpretation. The medieval medical tradition, which viewed lovesickness as a very real physical ailment, was as central to the characterisation of Troilus as was the tradition of courtly love, which was in any case partly borne out of the medical tradition popular throughout the Middle Ages.[37] However, R. M. Lumiansky rejects the traditional diagnosis of lovesickness, instead arguing for the narrator as a mourner,[38] and J. Burke Severs argues that we find no evidence whatsoever in the text that the narrator is a lover.[39] John M. Hill suggests that, instead of lovesickness, the narrator suffers from an imbalance of humours referred to in the Middle

---

36　Ibid., 45.
37　Mary Wack "Lovesickness in Troilus", *Pacific Coast Philology* 19 (1984): 55–73. See also Mary Wack, *Lovesickness in the Middle Ages: The Viaticum and its Commentaries*. Philadelphia: University of Pennsylvania Press, 1990 for editions and commentary of some of the medical texts that spread this tradition throughout Europe.
38　"The Bereaved Narrator in Chaucer's the *Book of the Duchess*", *Tennessee Studies in Literature* 9 (1959): 5–17.
39　"Chaucer's Self-Portrait in the *Book of the Duchess*", *Philological Quarterly* 43 (1964): 27–39.

Ages as "head melancholy".[40] Nor is Chaucer's narrator the only dreamer to suffer from insomnia in medieval dream-vision poetry; Peter Brown notes that in many dream visions dreamers must endure insomnia before the dream can begin;[41] this sleeplessness, Brown argues, produces within them a sense of anxiety that accompanies their parallel anxiety about something in the world.[42]

However, the narrator does not seem particularly anxious. He is ambiguous about the cause of his sickness, and there is no impression of alarm or fear. Although men might ask him why he suffers this insomnia

> Myselven can not telle why
> The sothe; but trewly, as I gesse,
> I holde hit be a sicknesse
> That I have suffred this eight yeer;
> And yet my boote is never the ner,
> For there is phisicien but oon
> That may me hele; but that is don. (34–40)

The phrase "phisicien but oon" might hint at lovesickness, or, as Severs suggests, this "oon" might be God and the problem might be one of spiritual transgression.[43] Yet this proposition, like the theory of lovesickness, finds little basis in the poem itself. The fact of the matter is that the text itself does not reveal the specific nature of the narrator's sickness, except that it is some sort of emotional stress – the melancholy of line 23.

While inviting multiple responses to his illness, the narrator suggests that the issue is really quite trivial:

> Passe we over [the cause of the narrator's sickness] untill eft;
> That wil not be mot nede be left;
> Our first mater is good to kepe. (41–3)

---

40 "The *Book of the Duchess*, Melancholy and That Eight-Year Sickness", *Chaucer Review* 9 (1974): 35–50. It should be noted that Chaucer does use the word "melancolye" to describe his ailment (l.23).
41 *On the Borders of Middle English Dream Visions*. Oxford: Oxford University Press, 1999: 29.
42 Ibid., 30–2.
43 "Chaucer's Self-Portrait", 27–39.

At first glance this passage seems to be a mere transition where Chaucer admits that he has got a bit off-track and must turn to the point of the poem. In fact, this is a highly complex rhetorical move. Chaucer employs *amplificatio* to describe the symptoms of his ailment, but uses *abbreviatio* to describe its causes. From a hermeneutic standpoint, this focus provides a superficial knowledge of the narrator, giving Gaunt a limited perspective from which to judge him. The narrator is thus, by being ambiguously melancholic, in the perfect position to console the Man in Black without appearing to have, to use Bahr's phrase, "superior emotional wisdom". For a consolatory poem written for a social superior, no rhetorical move could have been more appropriate. Chaucer's lack of specificity allows John of Gaunt the freedom to see the narrator as a lovesick lover or as a mourner. In either case, the narrator's situation would have been identifiable with Gaunt's own, while its vagueness allowed Chaucer space to defer. It is as if Chaucer is here telling Gaunt that he can only partially empathise with him because of his own insensitivity, while allowing Gaunt interpretative authority over himself if the nobleman conflates the narrator with the poet.

Chaucer opens his narrator's personality to an almost endless range of possible interpretations, as can be seen from twentieth century readings of the figure. Thomas Garbáty describes the narrator's behaviour in the poem as "reasonable", because he undermines the severity of Gaunt's grief by applying rational solutions to an emotional problem.[44] James R. Kreuzer and Bertrand H. Bronson also find him a tactful and understanding figure.[45] For Charles Muscatine, however, the narrator is comical, and his naiveté is deferential rhetoric on Chaucer's part, for it "serves to define the distance between poet and patron, between the Narrator and the elevated objects of his narration [i.e., John of Gaunt and Blanche]".[46] And in Muscatine's reading, this is deference only if the narrator is the rhetorical representation of

---

44   Thomas J. Garbáty, "The Degredation of Chaucer's 'Geffrey'" *PMLA* 89 (1974): 97–104, at 98–9.
45   James R. Kreuzer, "The Dreamer in the *Book of the Duchess*", *PMLA* 66 (1951): 543–7 and Bertrand H. Bronson, "The *Book of the Duchess* Re-Opened", *PMLA* 67 (1952): 863–81.
46   Charles Muscatine, *Chaucer and the French Tradition*. Berkeley, Calif.: University of California Press, 1957: 104.

Chaucer the man. Even if he is a simpleton or too literal-minded, this need not mean that he was intended to be understood as a fiction entirely removed from the figure of Chaucer himself, as the poem ends by emphasising *the poet's* inability to understand Gaunt's plight and, more importantly, to console (see below).

The narrator's ambiguous sickness foreshadows the narrator's superficial reading of the Alcyone and Seys story that immediately follows. This tale of two lovers separated by death and later reunited when they are turned into two halcyons has its ultimate source in Ovid's *Metamorphoses* (XI.410–749) and is entirely appropriate for the context of the poem's reception as Chaucer's appeal to Gaunt's emotions. A parallel context surrounds Guillaume de Machaut's *Dit de la fonteinne amoreuse,* where the Alcyone and Ceyx myth is retold in a condensed summary:

> Et de si long ne li porroie dire
>   Qu'elle m'affame
> Des tres dous biens amoureus, si qu'eslire
> De mes meschiés ne saroie le pire,
> Car en mon fait ne voy rien qui n'empire
>   Toudis, par m'ame.
> Si me couvient autre voie querir,
> Se savoir vueil a quel fin puis venir
> De ceste amour que je vueil maintenir,
>   Qui tout me mine.
> Quant roy Ceis fist fortune perir
> Dedens la mer, il le couvint morir,
> Mais tant ne pot Alchioinne enquerir,
>   Qui fu roÿne,
> Ne faire tant a devin n'a devinne
> Qu'elle en peüst savoir le voir, et si ne
> Faisoit que li querir seur la marine,
>   Car, sans mentir,
> Elle l'amoit plus que rien d'amour fine:
> Ses crins tiroit et batoit sa poitrine
> Et pour s'amour seur lit ne soubs courtine
>   Ne pot dormir.

And from so far away I would not be able to tell her that she is starving me of the very sweet, good things of love, so that I would not know how to pick out the worst of my griefs, for in my predicament I cannot see anything which, by my soul, does not grow worse all the time.

So I must find some other way, if I wish to know how I can advance this love that I want to keep up, and which quite destroys me. When Fortune caused King Ceyx to perish in the sea, he had to die. But Alcyone, who was his queen, could never enquire enough, or enough consult soothsayers, that she knew the truth of what had happened. And so she had him searched for on the sea; for in truth, she loved him more than anything, with a most pure love. (*La Fonteinne amoureuse* 533–54)[47]

Machaut was writing for Jean, duke of Berry, on the occasion of the duke's departure to England in 1360, where he would be held hostage under the terms of the Treaty of Brétigny. Because Berry would be separated from his recently wedded wife, Jeanne d'Armagnac, the context of this poem is comparable to that of the *Book of the Duchess*. In both cases, the poets wrote a text that on the one hand mourns the loss of a love and on the other ennobles the lovers and their separation by situating their relationship in courtly and classical traditions. Both also directly address the nobleman's pain while giving his suffering a poetic voice that becomes a form of consolation.

While Chaucer tells the story of Alcyone through his narrator, Machaut relates it through the nobleman of the poem who is to be conflated with Jean of Berry.[48] By allowing Jean to voice this myth, Machaut gives his audience the impression that the duke was a lucid, passionate, and chivalrous knight, well versed in the traditions of classical myth and courtly love while the explicit parallel between the two couples humanises and ennobles Jean's loss.

This ennobling parallel is more concealed in Chaucer's retelling. Whereas Machaut "builds on the consoling theme in Ovid's reunion of the royal pair after their metamorphosis into birds" to produce a story that "centers on comfort through communication",[49] Chaucer

47   All quotations of Machaut are from *Œuvres de Guillaume de Machaut*, 3 vols., Ernest Hoepffner (ed.). Paris: Librairie de Firmin-Didot et Companie, 1921. The translation is B. A. Windeatt's (in *Chaucer's Dream Poetry: Sources and Analogues*. Cambridge: D. S. Brewer, 1982).
48   He is named Jean, duke of Berry in an anagram at ll.45–54.
49   Kay Gilliland Stevenson, "Readers, Poets and Poems within the Poem", *Chaucer Review* 24 (1989): 1–19, at 4.

presents the story only as the narrator's inspiration to sacrifice his bedding to get to sleep:

> Yif I ne had red and take kep
> Of this tale next before.
> And I wol telle yow wherfore:
> For I ne myghte, for bote ne bale,
> Slepe or I had red thys tale
> Of this dreynte Seys the kyng
> And of the goddes of slepyng. (224–30)

For the narrator, the tale becomes a source of learning, even if it is a courtly story of love lost and regained easily conflated with the story of the Black Knight that follows. Kay Gilliland Stevenson likens the narrator's use of the story to "reading Homer to learn about chariot-driving or physic".[50] Although he describes reading as "pleye", his act of reading a book of love becomes an edifying exercise.

The narrator's inability to catch the courtly theme of the story might be understandable if he were new to the world of books, but we learn at the beginning of the poem that he is a habitual reader:

> So when I saw I might not slepe
> Til now late this other night
> Upon my bed I sat upright
> And bad oon reche me a book,
> A romaunce, and he it me tok
> To rede and drive the night away;
> For me thoughte it better play
> Then playe either at ches or tables. (44–51)

Because he approaches the book with a pragmatic desire – namely, to sleep – J. J. Anderson argues that the narrator does not have "any interest in books or reading as such, but [he approaches the text] in order to help him to sleep, as an alternative to chess or backgammon".[51] But to my mind the phrase "better play" suggests that the nar-

---

50 "Readers, Poets and Poems within the Poem", 4.
51 "The Narrators in the *Book of the Duchess* and the *Parlement of Fowls*", *Chaucer Review* 26 (1992): 219–35, at 221.

rator does have at least a qualified interest in reading; he is more a reader than a courtly lover within the duality that Chaucer makes by juxtaposing the worlds of readers and the aristocracy, metonymically referred to here in the images of chess and backgammon.[52]

The narrator's reading habits also distance him from interpersonal interaction. Since he reads privately and silently, his reading is not a public, inclusive affair, a point that Chaucer emphasises by presenting his narrator as more removed from the world than he himself was. We are invited to imagine Chaucer propped up in his bed alone, reading in his bedchamber away from the world (the "oon" whom the narrator asks to fetch a book must be understood as a servant of some sort, not a wife or lover).[53]

The narrator's subsequent sacrifice of his bedding to Morpheus is absurd comedy at its most naked, which Chaucer emphasises by calling the sacrifice a "game" (238). The comedy of this scene is augmented by the fact that his sacrifice actually works. His explicit use of the Alcyone and Seys myth is categorically non-courtly, characterising the narrator, and himself by extension, as outsiders to the courtly community, while the implicit connection between Alcyone and Gaunt dignifies the nobleman's loss. Chaucer and his narrator appear incapable of appreciating the beauty of the story of Alcyone and Seys on its own, let alone the analogue to Gaunt, while the poem's audience appears a courtly community all the more by contrast when they recognise the connection between Gaunt and Alcyone. Paradoxically, by keeping the analogy implicit and subtle, Chaucer creates a sophisticated and moving literary conceit while appearing gauche and dim-witted.

In a discussion of the Alcyone and Ceyx section of *Book of the Duchess*, there is much room to speak of firsts. This redaction is Chaucer's first attempt to retell an Ovidian tale in what becomes his first lengthy, completed narrative poem. It is also the first adaptation of Ovid

---

52   The various meanings and symbolic significance of chess to the aristocracy in the Middle Ages has been well studied, as I discuss below. For a good general treatment of medieval games, see Compton Reeves, *Pleasures and Pastimes in Medieval England*. Oxford: Oxford University Press, 1995: 73–88.
53   Although Chaucer was married at the time, the "oon" is referred to by the masculine pronoun "he" in line 48, so this person cannot be his wife Philippa.

to English poetry, so it is not much of an exaggeration to say that the enormous influence Ovid has had on English poetry begins here. Chaucer chose to retell a story from the *Metamorphoses,* and he would return to this work many times throughout his lifetime, while the *Heroides, Ars Amatoria,* and *Remedia Amoris* are rarely mentioned and still more rarely transfigured into his poetry. Chaucer was not alone in this selectivity; French poets of the thirteenth and fourteenth centuries seem to have likewise been most interested in the *Metamorphoses,* although the indirect influence of Ovid's other works, especially *Ars Amatoria,* on the love poetry of medieval France cannot go unnoticed.

These French poets developed a literary tradition of transforming Ovid for different ends, and their techniques bear relevance to Chaucer, who encountered Ovid not only in the Latin original, but also through the French appropriators. For *Book of the Duchess*, Jean de Meun and Guillaume de Machaut offered two approaches to Ovidian mythography which greatly vary from each other. While Chaucer's debt to the *Roman de la rose* is obvious here, it does not seem that Meun's use of Ovid inspired Chaucer's own adaptation (in any case, Guillaume de Lorris's section of the *Roman* was more influential to *Book of the Duchess* than Meun's more allegorical continuation).

Perhaps Meun's moralistic use of Ovid did not provide Chaucer with useful material for his own poetic circumstance. Meun could not help but reject Ovid's impropriety, such as when he attacks Orpheus for his sinful homosexuality:

> Ou leur semence vait a perte,
> Ne ja n'i tendront dreite rue,
> Ainz vont bestournant la charrue,
> E conferment leur regles males
> Par excepcions anormales,
> Quant Orpheüs veulent ensivre,
> Qui ne sot arer ne escrivre
> Ne forgier en la dreite forge,
> Penduz seit il par mi la gorge !
> Quant teus regles leur controuva,
> Vers Nature mal se prouva.

> Those who will never keep to the straight track, but instead go overturning the plow, who confirm their evil rules by abnormal exceptions when they want to

follow Orpheus (he did not know how to plow or write or forge in the true forge – may he be hanged by the throat! – when he showed himself so evil toward Nature by contriving such rules for them). (19646–56)[54]

In Ovid's account, Orpheus loses Eurydice twice – once on Earth and once in Hades, when he attempts to bring her back to Earth – and the grief of this double-loss becomes too much for him to bear. As a result, he finds comfort in the love of boys:

> Orantem frustraque iterum transire volentem
> portitor arcuerat: septem tamen ille diebus
> squalidus in ripa Cereris sine munere sedit;
> cura dolorque animi lacrimaeque alimenta fuere.
> esse deos Erebi crudeles questus, in altam
> se recipit Rhodopen pulsumque aquilonibus Haemum.
> Tertius aequoreis inclusum Piscibus annum
> finierat Titan, omnemque refugerat Orpheus
> femineam Venerem, seu quod male cesserat illi,
> sive fidem dederat; multas tamen ardor habebat
> iungere se vati, multae doluere repulsae
> ille etiam Thracum populis fuit auctor amorem
> in teneros transferre mares citraque iuventam
> aetatis breve ver et primos carpere flores.

Orpheus prayed and wished in vain to cross the Styx a second time, but the keeper drove him back. Seven days he sat there on the bank in filthy rags and with no taste of food. Care, anguish of soul, and tears were his nourishment. Complaining that the gods of Erebus were cruel, he betook himself to high Rhodope and wind-swept Haemus.

Three times had the sun finished the year and come to watery Pisces; and Orpheus had shunned all love of womankind, whether because it had gone so ill with him, or because he had so given his troth. Still, many women felt a passion for the bard; many grieved for their love repulsed. He set the example for the peoples of Thrace of giving his love to tender boys, and enjoying the springtime and first flower of their youth. (X.72–85)[55]

---

54   I am using Ernest Langlois's edition of *Le Roman de la rose*, 5 vols. Paris: Libraire de Firmin-Didot, 1914. The translation is by Charles Dahlberg, *The Romance of the Rose*. Princeton, NJ: Princeton University Press, 1971.

55   All Latin quotations and English translations of the *Metamorphoses* are from Frank Justus Miller's Loeb edition (*Metamorphoses* 2 vols. Cambridge, Mass.: Harvard University Press, 1946).

Jean de Meun's moral denigration of Orpheus' homosexuality, at odds with Ovid's more favourable attitude, is hardly surprising.

Yet we should be surprised to find Chaucer's insistence not to moralise Ovid, even in his descriptions of the first homosexual. In the *House of Fame*, we find the image of Orpheus as an artist:

> Ther herde I pleyen on an harpe,
> That sowned bothe wel and sharpe,
> Orpheus ful craftely (*House of Fame* III.1201–3)

Chaucer also invokes Orpheus and Eurydice in Criseyde's tragic complaint on the eve of her ransom to the Greeks, when she will be separated from Troilus:

> Myn herte and ek the woful goost therinne
> Byquethe I with youre spirit to compleyne
> Eternaly, for they shal nevere twynne;
> For though in erthe ytwynned be we tweyne,
> Yet in the feld of pite, out of peyne,
> That highte Elisos, shal we ben yfeere,
> As Orpheus and Erudice, his feere. (*Troilus and Criseyde* IV.785–91)

We cannot expect this to stem from a tolerance towards homosexuality – Chaucer's description of the Pardoner in the *General Prologue* portrays sexual abnormality as a mark of inner vice (I.688–91). The reason lies elsewhere, and it has much to do with Chaucer's sense of what is meaningful in Ovid, what is worth emphasising, and what is worth bringing to the English cultural milieu. Chaucer's adaptations of Orpheus seem to have been much more inspired by the Boethian perspective on the myth, which emphasises Orpheus' sorrow and the destructiveness of unbridled passion:

> But what is he that may yeven a lawe to loverys? Love is a grettere lawe and a strengere to hymself thanne any lawe that men mai yyven. Allas! Whanne Orpheus and his wif weren almest at the termes of the nyght (*that is to seyn, at the laste boundes of helle*), Orpheus lokede abakward on Erudyce his wif, and lost hire, and was deed.
>
> This fable apertenith to yow alle, whosoevere desireth or seketh to lede his thought into the sovereyn day, that is to seyn, to cleernesse of sovereyn good.

> For whoso that evere be so overcomen that he ficche his eien into the put of helle, that is to seyn, whoso sette his thoughtes in erthly thinges, al that evere he hath drawen of the noble good celestial he lesith it, whanne he looketh the helles, that is to seyn, into lowe thinges of the erthe. (*Boece* Book III, Verse 12)

In *Book of the Duchess*, Orpheus is simply the "god of melodye" (569), and keeps company with Ovid, Dedealus, Hippocrates, and Galen – authorities of antiquity, whose dignity and respectability are the *sine qua non* for their presence in the poem.

It is also possible that Jean de Meun's moral condemnation of Ovid's pagan attitudes towards sinners such as Orpheus was rendered obsolete by a much more cogent and popular moral adaptation of Ovid: the early fourteenth century *Ovide moralisé*.[56] Instead of a direct condemnation of Ovid, the author of the *Moralisé* intertwines a translation of Ovid's *Metamorphoses* with a moralising allegory of the story just told. Yet as a source for vernacular poetry, the *Moralisé* was hardly successful and its influence on Chaucer is questionable.[57] The parallels we can find between the two might be echoes of Machaut's adaptations of the *Moralisé* to his own work. If Chaucer did refer to the *Moralisé*, it was more to help him decipher Ovid's Latin than to subsume the author's moral exegesis. Similarly, although Machaut used the *Moralisé*, he disregarded the text's allegorising moral framework that was added to contain Ovid's work. Like Chaucer, Machaut's use of Ovid is by no means moralistic; often he uses Ovid to dignify his own poetry and its subjects.

---

[56] An exact date for the poem is not known, but it was written before 1328; however, it does not seem to have been widely known until Guillaume de Machaut's use of it in the mid-fourteenth century; see *Ovide moralisé*, C. de Boer, (ed.). Amsterdam: Johannes Müller, 1915: 9–11.

[57] For opposing views on this issue, see Helen Cooper, "Chaucer and Ovid: A Question of Authority" in *Ovid Renewed: Ovidian Influences on Literature and Art from the Middle Ages to the Twentieth Century*, Charles Martindale (ed.). Cambridge: Cambridge University Press, 1988: 71–88, at 74–5 and John Fyler, *Chaucer and Ovid*. New Haven, Conn.: Yale University Press, 1979: 17. A. J. Minnis writes that Chaucer knew the *Ovide moralisé* and Bersuire's *Ovidius moralizatus*, but Chaucer's "interest was (to apply Bersuire's categories) literal and historical but rarely, if ever, spiritual or moral" (*Chaucer and Pagan Antiquity*. Cambridge: D. S. Brewer, 1982: 16).

Machaut's adaptation of the Alcyone and Ceyx story, which came to serve as an example for Chaucer, well illustrates this point. Ovid's stories of metamorphosis are often tales of tragic loss caused by transformation; this myth is different, since the final transformation of Alcyone and Ceyx into birds is a redemption from Ceyx' death and Alcyone's subsequent lamentation and sorrow enacted by pitying gods:

>   adiacet undis
> facta manu moles, quae primas aequoris undas
> frangit et incursus quae praedelassat aquarum.
> insilit huc, mirumque fuit potuisse: volabat
> percutiensque levem modo natis aera pennis
> stringebat summas ales miserabilis undas,
> dumque volat, maesto similem plenumque querellae
> ora dedere sonum tenui crepitantia rostro.
> ut vero tetigit mutum et sine sanguine corpus,
> dilectos artus amplexa recentibus alis
> frigida nequiquam duro dedit oscula rostro.
> senserit hoc Ceyx, an vultum motibus undae
> tollere sit visus, populus dubitabat, at ille
> senserat: et, tandem superis miserantibus, ambo
> alite mutantur; fatis obnoxius isdem
> tunc quoque mansit amor nec coniugiale solutum
> foedus in alitibus: coeunt fiuntque parentes,
> perque dies placidos hiberno tempore septem
> incubat Alcyone pendentibus aequore nidis.
> tunc iacet unda maris: ventos custodit et arcet
> Aeolus egressu praestatque nepotibus aequor.

Near by the water was a mole built which broke the first onslaught of the waters, and took the force of the rushing waves. Thither she ran and leaped into the sea; 'twas a wonder that she could; she flew and, fluttering through the yielding air on sudden wings, she skimmed the surface of the water, a wretched bird. And as she flew, her croaking mouth, with long slender beak, uttered sounds like one in grief and full of complaint. But when she reached the silent, lifeless body, she embraced the dear limbs with her new-found wings and strove vainly to kiss the cold lips with her rough bill. Whether Ceyx felt this, or whether he but seemed to lift his face by the motion of the waves, men were in doubt. But he did feel it. And at last, through the pity of the gods, both changed to birds. Though thus they suffered the same fate, still even thus their love remained, nor were their conjugal bonds loosened because of their feathered shape. Still do they mate and rear their young; and for seven peaceful days in the winter season Alcyone broods upon her nest floating upon the surface of the waters. At such a time the waves of the sea are still; for Aeolus guards his winds and forbids them to go abroad and for his grandsons' sake gives peace upon the sea. (XI.728-48)

In Machaut's version, Juno responds to Alcyone's complaint by turning the two into birds (*Fontienne* 648-98). This added detail suggests that the complaint can effect change; the lord's complaint becomes a plea for help in the hope of changing the inevitable. The ostensive reason why the lord chooses to retell this story is made clear in his later comment that he cannot sleep because he has no joy and cannot rest (l.703). In this he manifests the typical symptoms of lovesickness, as medieval medicine understood the "disease", and this detail emphasises the lord's love and the pathos of his situation. Of course it is obvious that Machaut retells this story to invite parallels between Jean, duc de Berry and Alcyone, and the myth is, as I have mentioned, appropriate. Alcyone's fears provide a suitable expression of the lord's anxieties, while her reunion with Ceyx provides hope for the knight and his lady; at the end of the poem, further literary comforts and verbal consolations provide the two with confidence in their mutual love, which gives the poem its happy ending.

Unlike Machaut's adaptation, Chaucer's version of the story of "Alcione and Seys the kyng and of the goddes of slepyng" has its touches of comedy, as does his version of the meeting between Juno's messenger (who is Iris in the *Metamorphoses*) and Morpheus:

> This messager com fleynge faste
> And cried, "O, how! Awake anoon!"
> Hit was for noght; there herde hym non.
> "Awake!" quod he, "whoo ys lyth there?"
> And blew his horn ryght in here eere,
> And cried "Awaketh!" wonder hyë.
> This god of slep with hys oon yë
> Cast up, and axed, "Who clepeth ther?" (178-85)

The sleepy God of Sleep is a quaint touch, and the squawking imperatives of the messenger ("Awake anoon!", "Awake!", "Awaketh!") are a subtle onomatopoetic allusion to the birds that find no place in

Chaucer's version of the story (more on this later). In Ovid's account, this meeting is given much more grandeur:

> Quo simul intravit manibusque obstantia virgo
> Somnia dimovit, vestis fulgore reluxit
> sacra domus, tardaque deus gravitate iacentes
> vix oculos tollens iterumque iterumque relabens
> summaque percutiens nutanti pectora mento
> excussit tandem sibi se cubitoque levatus,
> quid veniat, (cognovit enim) scitatur, at illa:
> "Somne, quies rerum, placidissime, Somne, deorum,
> pax animi, quem cura fugit, qui corpora duris
> fessa ministeriis mulces reparasque labori."

> When the maiden entered there and with her hands brushed aside the dream-shapes that blocked her way, the awesome house was lit up with the gleaming of her garments. Then the god, scarce lifting his eyelids heavy with the weight of sleep, sinking back repeatedly and knocking his breast with his nodding chin, at last shook himself free of himself and, resting on an elbow, asked her (for he recognized her) why she came. And she replied: "O Sleep, thou rest of all things, Sleep, mildest of the gods, balm of the soul, who puttest care to flight, soothest our bodies worn with hard ministries, and preparest them for toil again." (XI.616–25)

Chaucer chooses to omit these descriptions of sleep's restorative powers and the God of Sleep's magnanimous service to mankind, even though the story of Alcyone and Seys is seemingly mentioned only because it gave the narrator inspiration to cure the sleeplessness which had plagued him for eight years (37), and which he fears will cause his death (24). Instead, Chaucer translates Ovid into something close to slapstick, preparing the audience for the comedy of the narrator's response.[58]

Chaucer does not comment further on the Ovidian tale, but his larger purpose would have been obvious to anyone familiar with Gaunt's situation – to invite comparisons between Gaunt and Alcyone. It is in this aspect of the adaptation that Chaucer appears most delicate. Unlike Machaut, Chaucer excludes the reunion of Alcyone and

---

58 Chaucer returns to the God of Sleep in the *House of Fame* (I.69–76), where the God and his dwelling are given more dignity, although not the praise of Ovid.

Ceyx found in Ovid, perhaps partly because the only reunion available to Gaunt would be his death, an event which Chaucer was careful not to invoke. Also central to this omission is the potential implications such a suggestion would have had for Gaunt's position in English society; since the metamorphosis of Alcyone into a halcyon allows her a reunion with her lost lover only at the expense of her humanity and her involvement in human affairs, the parallel this ending would invite for Gaunt might appear a political proclamation. Chaucer is quick to avoid these matters, and uses as a ruse his narrator's apathy to Alcyone's grief:

> With that hir [Alcyone] eyen up she casteth
> And saw noght. "Allas!" quod she for sorwe,
> And deyede within the thridde morwe.
> But what she sayede more in that swow
> I may not telle yow as now;
> Hyt were to longe for to dwelle.
> My first matere I wil yow telle,
> Wherfore I have told this thyng
> Of Alcione and Seys the kyng,
> For thus moche dar I saye wel:
> I had be dolven everydel
> And ded, ryght thurgh defaute of slep,
> Yif I ne had red and take kep
> Of this tale next before. (212–25)

Later, the narrator will endure lengthy complaints from the Black Knight, betraying the apathy he here conveys, while, paradoxically, his seeming disinterest in Alcyone's cries of pity and sorrow prepares the audience for his later inability to comprehend the Black Knight's pain, and while allowing Chaucer to escape any political implications the Ovidian metamorphosis might have.

A more personal sympathy also inspired Chaucer's narrative choices. The level of intimacy between Alcyone and Seys is much greater in Chaucer's version, where no other human being speaks or is even mentioned (the only other characters to speak are divine). In Ovid's telling of the story, Alcyone and Ceyx begin very much in the public world of politics; Ceyx is introduced as the ruler of Trochis, where Peleus has come as a supplicant. Chaucer, on the other hand, makes no mention of Seys' political position other than that he was a king (62), and the men and women of his kingdom are never mentioned. Similarly, Chaucer omits the details provided by Ovid of Ceyx' motivations to travel – he plans to search for Peleus and visit the oracles of the Clarian god. All of this occurs only after Ceyx had prepared himself and his men for war:

> induere arma viros violentaque sumere tela
> rex iubet Oetaeus; cum quis simul ipse parabat
> ire, sed Alcyone coniunx excita tumultu
> prosilit et nondum totos ornata capillos
> disicit hos ipsos colloque infusa mariti,
> mittat ut auxilium sine se, verbisque precatur
> et lacrimis, animasque duas ut servet in una.

> The Oetaean king bade his men put on their armour and take their deadly spears in hand, and at the same time was making ready to go with them himself. But his wife, Alcyone, roused by the loud outcries, came rushing out of her chamber, her hair not yet all arranged, and, sending this flying loose, she threw herself upon her husband's neck, and begged him with prayers and tears that he would send aid but not go himself, and so save two lives in one. (XI.382–8)

Alcyone's concerns are not met with the comforts of a loving husband; they come from Peleus, who insists that he will not let Ceyx or his men die for his life – a promise fulfilled, although Ceyx' obstinacy is not hindered, and he leaves because of worry for his brother and his kingdom.

In Chaucer's version, we get none of this. Instead, we are briefly told that

> So it befil thereafter soone
> This king wol wenden over see.
> To tellen shortly, whan that he
> Was in the see thus in this wise,
> Such a tempest gan to rise
> That brak her mast and made it falle,
> And clefte her ship, and dreinte hem alle,
> That never was founde, as it telles,
> Bord ne man, ne nothing elles.
> Right thus this king Seys loste his lif. (66–75)

Chaucer then devotes his energies to Alcyone's grief, the God of Sleep, and the message that he will carry to Alcyone. However, as I have already discussed, his attention towards her grief wanes with a lethargy that is contradicted by his later attempts to heal the Black Knight's grief and hear his story.

In the dream conversation between Alcyone and Morpheus in the guise of Seys, we see the added intimacy of Chaucer's version of events most clearly. In Ovid's original, Morpheus gives Alcyone the news of her husband's death and instructs her to mourn like a dutiful wife:

> "agnoscis Ceyca, miserrima coniunx,
> an mea mutata est facies nece? respice: nosces
> inveniesque tuo pro coniuge coniugis umbram!
> nil opis, Alcyone, nobis tua vota tulerunt!
> occidimus! falso tibi me promittere noli!
> nubilus Aegaeo deprendit in aequore navem
> Auster et ingenti iactatam flamine solvit,
> oraque nostra tuum frustra clamantia nomen
> inplerunt fluctus. – non haec tibi nuntiat auctor
> ambiguus, non ista vagis rumoribus audis:
> ipse ego fata tibi praesens mea naufragus edo.
> surge, age, da lacrimas lugubriaque indue nec me
> indeploratum sub inania Tartara mitte!"

> "Do you recognize your Ceyx, O most wretched wife? or is my face changed in death? Look on me! You will know me then and find in place of husband your husband's shade. No help, Alcyone, have your prayers brought to me: I am dead. Cherish no longer your vain hope of me. For stormy Auster caught my ship on the Aegean sea and, tossing her in his fierce blasts, wrecked her there. My lips, calling vainly upon your name, drank in the waves. And this tale no uncertain messenger brings to you, nor do you hear it in the words of vague report; but I myself, wrecked as you see me, tell you of my fate. Get you up, then, and weep for me; put on your mourning garments and let me not go unlamented to the cheerless land of shades." (XI.658–70)

The attention to her clothing bespeaks a concern that her mourning be conspicuous, and that Ceyx' memory be remembered; the concern that Alcyone must mourn her husband publicly is a wish that his memory be respected. If these were in fact the words of Ceyx, he would seem selfish and insensitive. But as the words of Morpheus, they show a divine admiration and respect for Ceyx, which should not surprise us, as he is one of the few characters of the *Metamorphoses* who acts not out of personal desire but for the honour of his family and country. At the same time, Ovid subverts the divine intention here, because Morpheus presents himself as Ceyx in what can be called no less than a willful deception; immediately after this speech, Ovid emphasises that it is the god and not the man speaking:

> adicit his vocem Morpheus, quam coniugis illa
> crederet esse sui (fletus quoque fundere veros
> visus erat), gestumque manus Ceycis habebat.
> ingemit Alcyone, lacrimans movet atque lacertos
> per somnum corpusque petens amplectitur auras.

> These words spoke Morpheus, and that, too, in a voice she might well believe her husband's; he seemed also to weep real tears, and had the very gesture of her Ceyx' hands. Alcyone groaned, shed tears, and in sleep seeking his arms and to clasp his body, held only air in her embrace. (XI.671–5)

Because such a monologue would hardly be appropriate for a man mourning the loss of his recently deceased wife, Chaucer changes this speech to its exact opposite:

> "My swete wyf,"
> "Awake! Let be your sorwful lyf,
> For in your sorwe there lyth no red;
> For, certes, swete, I am but ded.
> Ye shul me never on lyve yse.
> But, goode swete herte, that ye
> Bury my body, for such a tyde
> Ye mowe hyt fynde the see besyde;
> And farewel, swete, my worldes blysse!
> I praye God youre sorwe lysse.
> To lytel while oure blysse lasteth!" (201–11)

It was fitting to provide messages of abating grief and waning sorrow to John of Gaunt, and Chaucer here suggests a turn away from past loss and towards future life, which he underscores by adding that Alcyone died for grief in the lines that follow. Like the omission of the metamorphosis, the altered monologue and conclusion urge Gaunt to turn away from death and toward the community of the living around him without explicitly saying so.

After the narrator has cured his insomnia by appealing to the god of sleep, he immediately begins to dream. His windows are suddenly filled with stained glass depicting the story of Troy (321–31), and the walls hold the text and gloss of the *Romance of the Rose* (326–34). The narrator finds himself literally inside a romance, as if he has jumped into the type of book he was just reading in the waking world. Even in dreams, the narrator's head is full of thoughts about books.

Shortly after, the narrator stumbles upon a group lead by Emperor Octavian on a hunt for a hart, an obvious pun (344–86). He hears one of the party blow his horn and others talking about their hunt:

> And I herde goynge bothe up and doun
> Men, hors, houndes, and other thyng;
> And al men speken of hunting,
> How they wolde slee the hert with strengthe,
> And how the hert had upon lengthe
> So moche embossed – y not now what. (348–53)

Hunting was of course an activity for noblemen, and the hart was a noble animal. Yet on seeing this grand procession of "Men, hors, houndes, and other thyng" the narrator's reaction is one of exasperation, and he finally admits that he simply does not understand what the hunters are talking about.

The narrator then encounters a small puppy (a "whelp", as Chaucer calls it at 1.389), which is characterised as a helpless, innocent creature. The puppy, the narrator tells us, "fauned me as I stood" and it "koude no good" (389–90) – that is to say, it did not know what to do. This innocent animal

> com and crepte to me as lowe
> Ryght as hyt hadde me yknowe,
> Helde doun hys hed and joyned hys eres,
> And leyde al smothe doun hys heres.
> I wolde have kaught hyt, and anoon
> Hyt fledde and was fro me goon;
> And I hym folwed, and hyt forth wente

> Doun by a floury grene wente
> Ful thikke of gras, ful softe and swete. (391–9)

The narrator whimsically follows the whelp as it runs away towards the "floury greene", where the narrator meets and eventually converses with the Man in Black. The puppy, within the dream vision, is the one to introduce the narrator to the knight. The puppy's significance increases at this point, as it becomes clear that he is the narrator's dream guide. The puppy follows the tradition of Machaut's lion and Lorris's Idleness, and by contrast Chaucer's whelp appears a much more unassuming and playful guide.

The parallel structure of line 397 ("And I hym folwed, and hyt forth wente"), preceded by a syntactic interweaving of "I", "me", "hyt" and "whelp", implies a close, if not comparable, relationship between the naive and innocent narrator and puppy, who are both lost in a dream world that is incomprehensible to both of them. And like the puppy, the narrator is at a loss when he stumbles upon the Black Knight:

> I stalked even unto hys bak,
> And there I stood as stille as ought,
> That, soth to saye, he saw me nought (458–60)

While the "wel-farynge knight" sits "even upryght" (451–2) and makes his complaint, the narrator stands awkwardly behind him. This is a trick Chaucer learned from, among others, Machaut, who made his narrator a clumsy voyeur to the world of courtly love; in *La Fonteinne amoureuse* the narrator lies in bed when he overhears the knight's complaint, and in *Le Jugement dou Roy de Behaigne* the narrator, in order to overhear a knight and lady complain about their lost loves, crouches in the "embrunchiez qu'il ne me virent mie", "bushes so that they would not see me" (55).[59]

Both the puppy and the narrator are outsiders to the courtly worlds they half-belong to; they tag along with real courtly men,

---

[59] See A. C. Spearing, *The Medieval Poet as Voyeur*. Cambridge: Cambridge University Press, 1993 for an exploration of voyeurs in medieval love poetry, whose function is often to see and overhear secret love affairs.

whose involvement in hunting (in the case of Octavian) and love (in the case of the Man in Black) betray their superior and more respectable dispositions. Chaucer's narrator is an awkward figure from the moment he accidentally stumbles upon the Man in Black to the end of the dream. After he overhears the Man in Black's first complaint (475–86), he approaches the knight in the grove:

> Anoon therwith whan y sawgh this –
> He ferde thus evel there he set –
> I went and stood ryght at his fet,
> And grette hym; but he spak noght,
> But argued with his owne thoght,
> And in hys wyt disputed faste
> Why and how hys lyf myght laste. (500–6)

A mere hundred lines after the puppy scene, the narrator again describes himself in canine terms: he stands not in front of the Man in Black but at his feet.

The knight, in turn, does not notice the approach of his insignificant visitor, who is quick to defend the Man in Black's reaction, lest anyone consider him uncourtly:

> Hym thoughte hys sorwes were so smerte
> And lay so colde upon hys herte.
> So, throgh hys sorwe and hevy thoght,
> Made hym that he herde me noght;
> For he had wel nygh lost hys mynde,
> Thogh Pan, that men clepeth god of kynde,
> Were for hys sorwes never so wroth. (507–13)

"It is understandable if he did not notice me," the narrator says here, "because he had obviously nearly lost his wits for sorrow." In this the narrator steps outside of his usual obtuseness; he shows an understanding of the introversion that accompanies feelings of loss, despite the fact that, for the rest of the poem, he is characterised as a figure incapable of comprehending grief. This inconsistency might be abhorrent to a modern reader who expects whole, rounded characters, but it fits well with Chaucer's consistent rhetorical aim – to maintain a deferential voice and sympathetic ear to Gaunt and his sorrow.

The narrator reacts to being ignored by taking off his hat and greeting the Black Knight "as I best koude,/Debonayrly, and nothing lowed" (517–18). What exactly he says to the knight is not reported; instead, the Man in Black's response is brought to the fore:

> "I prey the, be not wroth.
> I herde the not, to seyn the soth,
> Ne I sawgh the not, syr, trewely." (519–21)

Both inside and outside the poem this polite apology is unnecessary; the knight and Gaunt are very much social superiors to the narrator and Chaucer, yet the Man in Black defers to the narrator in a most courtly manner. In this he seems to be the quintessential courtly knight.

This is clear flattery, and as a work of propaganda it convinces an audience to see Gaunt as an admirable and respectable nobleman, whose gentility extended beyond the expected. The suggestion here is a mere hint, but less subtle flattery also bolsters Chaucer's rhetoric. When the narrator first sees the Black Knight, he says that he thought this "wonder wel-farynge knight" to be "the age of foure and twenty yer" (452; 455), although Gaunt was already 28 when Blanche died – the lingering suggestion is that, even in mourning, Gaunt looks healthy and young. The Black Knight's complaint was, according to the narrator, "The moste pitee, the moste rowthe/That ever I herde" (465–6). If any doubt remains of Gaunt's passion for his first wife, this helps to quench it, while simultaneously complimenting Gaunt by trying to transfer the responsibility and credit for Chaucer's good poetry to the nobleman.

This is a familiar pose, which Chaucer surely took from Machaut. But unlike his French predecessor, Chaucer backs away from such a rhetorical move as soon as he begins it:

> for, by my trowthe,
> Hit was gret wonder that Nature
> Myght suffre any creature
> To have such sorwe and be not ded.
> Ful pitous pale and nothyng red,
> He sayd a lay, a maner song,
> Withoute noote, withoute song. (466–71)

He does not go so far as to say that the complaint is magnificent poetry, even if his previous hyperbole prepares one for such a proclamation. Instead, he concentrates on the depth of the Man in Black's sorrow, emphasising his distraught pity, not his lucidity. Here Chaucer escapes one of the traps of moving responsibility for good poetry to another person – ultimately, the poet really deserves the credit for the verse.

We find this problem in *La Fonteinne amoureuse* when the narrator moves to his ivory writing desk and transcribes the lover's complaint that he overhears. Afterwards, he marvels at the beauty of the passage:

>je lus de chief en chief
>La complainte qu'avoie escripte
>Pour vir s'il y avoit redite,
>Mais nes une n'en y trouvay;
>Et encor moult bien esprouvay
>Qu'il y avoit, dont j'eus merveilles,
>Cent rimes toutes despareilles.

>I read all of the complaint which I had written to see if he had repeated a rhyme, but there was not one to find, and I searched through and through and marvelled that there were one hundred different rhymes. (1046–52)

Machaut's wonder at the skill of his patron's complaint is too direct; in explicitly admiring the poetry that the patron "produced", his own pride of authorship comes to the forefront and the metafictional reality he has created deflates the flattery he attempts. By addressing the poetry itself, Machaut forces the audience to realise the fiction of the flattery because, ultimately, he himself was the one who composed those amazing one hundred rhymes. In this light, we may say that he used the *topoi* of self-deprecation and of transferring poetic skill as forms of flattery, but his poetic hubris[60] resulted in a contradictory

---

60   Proof that the pride of authorship we discover in Machaut's work is not an artificial construction with which to characterise his narrator is evident in two anomalies: firstly, his anagrams and, secondly, the simple fact that Machaut created an entire literary theory to supplement the reception of his works; as R. Barton Palmer observes, "his intention [was to] mediate the reception of his

metafictional implication that deflates this flattery. The trope is transparent, and the audience can easily work through the rhetoric to discover Machaut, in flattering his patron, is ultimately boasting of his own poetic deftness. Chaucer, I believe, would have seen this difficulty and, from the evidence of how he altered Machaut's shift of poetic responsibility, would have tried not to make the same error.

The Man in Black

Chaucer's emphasis on the Man in Black's grace as a lover is a consistent aspect of the poem, and in the knight's discourse there is a *gentilesse* that never wavers, even when he is faced with the awkward narrator. For example, the Black Knight uses the personal insufficiency topos to maintain a courtly humility:

> But which a visage had she [Whyte] thertoo!
> Allas, myn herte ys wonder woo
> That I ne kan discryven hyt!
> Me lakketh both Englyssh and wit
> For to undo hyt at the fulle;
> And eke my spirites be so dulle
> So gret a thing for to devyse.
> I have no wit that kan suffise
> To comprehende hir beaute.
> But thus moche dar I sayn, that she
> Was whit, rody, fressh, and lyvely hewed,
> And every day hir beaute newed. (895–906)

He repeatedly emphasises that he cannot describe his lady's beauty, although we know from the passages that immediately precede and follow this that he is more than able to describe her beauty in the con-

> works by establishing the particular intertextual network within which they were to be read" ("The Metafictional Machaut: Self-Reflexivity and Self-Mediation in the Two Judgment Poems", *Studies in the Literary Imagination* 20 (1987): 23–39, at 27.

ventional terms of the court. Significantly, the narrator does not make use of the personal insufficiency topos. We find little introversion or self-analysis in the narrator, which is consistent with his histrionic obtuseness both inside and outside the dream-world.

Much hangs on the narrator's inability to understand the Man in Black's complaint, and, at times, his failure is painful. For instance, he cannot comprehend why the Man in Black is so upset at losing a queen in a chess game:

> "At the ches with me she [Fortune – see l.618] gan to pleye;
> With hir false draughtes dyvers
> She staal on me and tok my fers.
> And whan I sawgh my fers awaye,
> Allas, I kouthe no lenger playe,
> But seyde, 'Farewel, swete, ywys,
> And farewell al that ever ther ys!'
> ...
> Allas, than am I overcome!
> For that ys doon ys not to come.
> I have more sorowe than Tantale."
> ...
> "A, goode sir," quod I, "say not soo!
> Have som pitee on your nature
> That formed yow to creature.
> Remembre yow of Socrates,
> For he ne counted nat thre strees
> Of noght that Fortune koude doo."
> "No," quod he, "I kan not soo."
> "Why so, good syr? Yis parde!" quod y;
> "Ne say noght soo, for trewely,
> Thogh ye had lost the ferses twelve,
> And ye for sorwe morderd yourselve,
> Ye sholde be dampned in this cas." (652–725)

The Man in Black patiently responds, "Thou wost ful lytel what thou menest;/I have lost more than thow wenest" (743–4), which prompts the narrator to ask "In what wyse, how, why, and wherfore/That ye have thus youre blysse lore" (747–8). The Man in Black proceeds to describe the white queen in great detail and to give a brief narrative of how he met her (749–1111). After this, the narrator directly asks to know more:

> "Now, goode syre," quod I thoo,
> "Ye han wel told me herebefore;
> Hyt ys no need to reherse it more,
> How ye sawe hir first, and where.
> But wolde ye tel me the manere
> To hire which was your firste speche –
> Therof I wolde yow beseche –
> And how she knewe first your thought,
> Whether ye loved hir or noght?
> And telleth me eke what ye have lore,
> I herde yow tell herebefore." (1126–36)

This bad-mannered request does not offend the Man in Black, even if it hurts him. He responds by repeating the refrain, "thow nost what thow menest;/I have lost more than thou wenest" (1137–8). The narrator has conjured the memory of the very first time the Man in Black spoke to his lady, and Chaucer humanises by recording his pang of remembrance while displaying yet again the narrator's insensitivity.

The narrator's reply appears rather callous:

> "What los ys that?" quod I thoo;
> "Nyl she not love yow? Ys hyt soo?
> Or have ye oght doon amys,
> That she hath left yow? Ys hyt this?
> For Goddes love, telle me al." (1139–43)

Without concern for the Black Knight, the narrator presses for more information, not bothering to ask if he has any objections. I find it difficult to describe this curiosity as tact; yet it does allow the Man in Black more space within the poem to continue his complaint while appearing courtly and graceful. In this sense, the narrator's obtuseness and impoliteness is Chaucer's tact; it allows a space within the mimetic world for the allegorical representation of John of Gaunt to memorialise the dead Blanche without appearing self-indulgent. At the same time, the narrator becomes the offensive scapegoat to be blamed for bringing up painful memories in the first place. The Black Knight responds to the narrator's inquisition with an almost inhuman patience, when he replies simply: "Before God and I shal [tell everything]" (1144).

In the continuation of the Man in Black's complaint, he gives another explicit hint that he has not only lost his lady, but that she has died:

> She *was* lady
> Of the body; she *had* the herte,
> And who hath that may not asterte. (1152–4, italics added)

This is still not clear enough for the narrator, who asks simply: "where is she now?", although the Black Knight has already answered this question more than once. To this, the Man in Black repeats his couplet and laments his loss anew (1299–307). Then the narrator prods him one final time:

> "Allas, sir, how? What may that be?"

To which the Man in Black finally says:

> "She ys ded!" "Nay!" "Yis, be my trouthe!" (1308–9)

The near-comic bathos of this passage is jarring and strange, not only because the understating, delicate courtliness of the Man in Black's preceding discourse is shattered, but also because this revelation should come as no surprise to the narrator, who should already know that the lady is dead from the first words he heard from the Black Knight:

> "I have of sorwe so gret won
> That joye gete I never non,
> Now that I see my lady bryght,
> Which I have loved with al my myght,
> Is fro me ded and ys agoon." (475–9)

Robert Watson notes that if the narrator "might have been tempted to misunderstand this statement as metaphorical, as has been suggested – the lady is 'dead' to the knight because she has deserted him – the concluding lines of the plaint clarify the matter by an apostrophe to

Death [at ll.481–6]".[61] If this was not enough, further clues are given throughout the Black Knight's complaint; lines 1124–5 explicitly state that the Man in Black has somehow lost his lady: "Nay, while I am alive her,/I nyl foryete hir never moo", and, when describing his lady's physical characteristics, he always uses past tense (for example, see ll.860, 866, 876, 941, 942). From beginning to end, the Black Knight makes it painstakingly obvious that the lady is dead.

In the light of this, I find it difficult to characterise the narrator in these moments as anything but obtuse; from the Man in Black's first lyric he learns that the lady has died, but he persists in asking if the knight has lost his lady in some other way later in the poem. How can the narrator be considered a tactful questioner if he forgot, did not pay attention to, or misunderstood this most explicit proclamation? His insensitivity is not malicious, however; the narrator botches the courtly conventions of his time because he is incapable of understanding the knight, as the Man in Black himself intimates in his thrice repeated refrain (ll.742–3, 1137–8, and 1305–6).

If the *Book of the Duchess* is a consolation poem, we might expect the narrator to respond to the last of the Man in Black's announcements of the lady's death with words of consolation, or at least with an expression of sympathy. Instead, the narrator obtusely says: "Is that youre los? Be God, hyt ys routhe!" (1310). Stevenson reads this line as "a final acknowledgment (bathetic or movingly honest) of the limitations of eloquence".[62] I would add that this limited eloquence is the narrator's, who displays an inherent inability to console at earlier points of the poem as well. After the Man in Black has told him of his "gret sorowe", as the narrator calls it (547), he says "by my trouthe, to make yow hool/I wol do al my power hool" (553–4). Chaucer adapted this line from Machaut's *Le Jugement dou Roy de Behaingne*, where a knight and a lady argue over who is suffering more for love, and in reply to the knight's request that the lady ignore her sadness to pay attention to him, she says: "Certes, sire, po me puis resjoir. Mais j'en feray mon pouir, sans mentir", "Certainly, sir, I can never be happy. But I will do all in my power, without a lie" (257–8).

---

61 "Dialogue and Invention", 112.
62 "Readers, Poets and Poems", 1.

When Chaucer puts the language of the court into the words of the narrator, they become discomforting and flaccid. The narrator qualifies his statement – he will do *his* best, which, as we have seen, is limited; even Chaucer's identical rhyme of "hool" seems to reinforce the narrator's and the poet's shortcomings. Inside the poem, the narrator has no words to console the Man in Black, implying that in the real world outside the poem Chaucer has no words to console John of Gaunt. It is impossible to separate the voice of the narrator from the voice of the poet in this passage – both express an incompetence and an inadequacy to comfort.

Chaucer ends his poem not by directing the audience's attention towards Blanche or even John of Gaunt, but by focusing on the narrator himself:

> Therwyth I awook myselve
> And fond me lyinge in my bed;
> And the book that I hadde red,
> Of Alcione and Seys the kyng,
> And of the goddes of slepyng,
> I fond hyt in myn hond ful even.
> Thoghte I, "Thys ys so queynt a sweven
> That I wol, be processe of tyme,
> Fonde to put this sweven in ryme
> As I kan best, and that anoon."
> This was my sweven; now hit ys doon. (1324–34)

As with the Alcyone/Seys story, the narrator here displays his incapacity to understand the depth of emotion contained within a touching story of emotional loss, and it is on this note that Chaucer ends the poem. The narrator leaves the Black Knight, Octavian's hunt, the beautiful, bountiful glade in May and the chamber decorated with the text of the *Romance of the Rose* to awake alone in his own chamber, isolated and removed from the courtly world, where the Black Knight remains in a state of unresolved sorrow, which the narrator deems "queynt". Chaucer ends the poem not by consoling John of Gaunt, nor by praising him, nor even by lamenting the death of Blanche, but by defining and mediating his own position in society.

The Allegory of Chess

Just as the narrator's lack of interest in chess distinguishes him from courtly society, so too is chess used to characterise the Man in Black and the late duchess as the dream vision unfolds. Chess in the late Middle Ages had many meanings. It was a diversion for the wealthy and a game of unusual intimacy, as it allows for only two players and was often played in private. The game itself is centred upon a political and social hierarchy which begins with the king. In his *Communeloquium*, John of Wales uses chess as an allegory for class distinctions.[63] Pamela Porter notes that "the religious, moral and political duties of the various social classes are presented in terms of chess" in the *Schachzal-Spil*, a late medieval allegorical treatise.[64] Chess was also, as Michael Camille observes, "[a]ssociated with warfare, mathematics, and male rationality".[65]

Chess was also a perfect metaphor for the battle of the sexes. Camille points out how a late fifteenth century chessboard from Burgundy alludes to the "game and the conquest of the lady in its delicately carved outer frame", which depicts on the one side armoured knights "with immensely long lances" and, on the other, "elegant ladies in their pointed Burgundian headdresses" dancing at a picnic. The chess set "literally spatializes gender difference across its playing-field, making every game of chess a literal war between the sexes".[66] Similarly, in British Library Add. MS 11616, we find a fifteenth century depiction of two royal figures, one male and one female, playing chess in an open field. Not only were the sexes at battle at the chessboard; they were also united in their mutual interest and the game at hand in an intimate setting.

63 The text is preserved in British Library Harley 2253.
64 Pamela F. Porter, *Courtly Love in Medieval Manuscripts*. London: British Library, 2003: 5.
65 *The Medieval Art of Love*. New York, NY: Abrams, 1998: 124.
66 Ibid. Compare the ca.1320 wood casket now held in Zürich, Schweizerisches Landesmuseum, which details two lovers playing chess (reproduced in ibid., 107) and the ca.1320 mirror case from Paris being held at the Musée du Louvre (reproduced in ibid., 124).

The central allegory of the *Book of the Duchess* is that of a chess game, in which the Man in Black, who is described by the narrator as a "wel-farynge knyght" (452), complains that he has lost his *fers*, or queen, in a game of chess against Fortune. The allegory Chaucer constructs in the poem is in some ways enigmatic. John of Gaunt was, of course, a military knight, and it is seemly that the Man in Black be called a knight as well. But by calling the Man in Black a black knight, Chaucer suggests the allegory of Blanche as a white queen and Gaunt as a black knight on the same side of a chess game.[67] However, the poem also makes it clear that the Man in Black is a chess player whose opponent is Fortune, thus providing confusing explicit and implicit allegorical clues in the poem.

W. W. Skeat was one of the first to attempt to alleviate our difficulties with the poem's chess allegory; in a note to line 655 ("And whan I saw my fers aweye"), Skeat writes that the loss of a queen is so crippling a blow that afterwards a player might "as well as give up the game".[68] However, Skeat's explanation was quickly discovered to be an anachronism. In 1948, Franklin Cooley explained that the queen in medieval chess was not the powerful piece it is today: "the medieval queen did not have much power, as she was limited to a move to an adjacent diagonal square".[69] In 1994, Margaret Connolly illuminated the rules of medieval chess further by citing a Caxton edition and translation of Jacobus de Cessolis' *Liber de moribus hominum et*

---

[67] Medieval rules of chess allowed for a black knight and a white queen to be on the same side of the chessboard. Margaret Connolly explains that chess pieces "were governed not by their own intrinsic color, but by the color of the square on which they stood" ("Chaucer and Chess", *Chaucer Review* 29 (1994): 40–4, at 41). Connolly quotes Jacobus de Cessolis' chess handbook: "he that is black in his propre siege is sette on the right side of the kyng and he that is why is sette on the lift side and ben callyd and named black and whyt but for no cause that they be so in substaunce of her propre colour, but for the colour of the places in whiche they ben sette" (ibid.). Thus both sides had a black and a white knight.

[68] *The Complete Works of Geoffrey Chaucer* vol. 1. Oxford: Clarendon Press, 1899: 480.

[69] "Two Notes on the Chess Terms in *The Book of the Duchess*", *MLN* 63 (1948): 30–5. For his source of the rules of medieval chess, Cooley quotes H. J. R. Murray's *History of Chess*. Oxford: Clarendon Press, 1918.

officiis nobilium ac popularium sive super ludo scacchorum as an example of the rules of chess that held currency in Chaucer's era:

> Her [the queen's] movements were restricted so that "whan she is meuyd ones out of her place she may not goo but fro one poynte to another, and yet couertly whether hit be forwarde or backward takyng or to be taken".[70]

The loss of a queen, then, was no great crippling blow, rendering the narrator's failure to understand why the Black Knight is so upset about losing his queen more sensible, according to Connolly, who goes on to argue that

> [t]he Dreamer fails then to understand the Black Knight's analogy, not through stupidity but because he is conversant with the rules of chess; his reaction at line 740–1: 'But ther is no man alyve her/ Wolde for a fers make this woo!' is therefore not unsympathetic, but merely an accurate statement.[71]

Guillemette Bolens and Paul Beckman Taylor add that any pawn can be promoted to a queen.[72]

But to emphasise the game of chess in the poem is, I think, to read like the narrator – too literally. In light of the real-world context of the poem, the development of the chess allegory becomes a symbol of Gaunt's personal loss, and Chaucer's intended audience would have concentrated on the allegory on this level. One point Connolly does not discuss is the narrator's reaction to the following complaint by the Man in Black:

> "For, also wys God yive me reste,
> I dar wel swere she [Fortune] took the beste.
> But through that draughte I have lorn
> My blysse; allas, that I was born!
> For evermore, y trowe trewly,
> For al my wille, my lust holly
> Ys turned; but yet, what to doone?

---

70 "Chaucer and Chess", 41.
71 Ibid., 42.
72 "Chess, Clocks, and Counsellors in Chaucer's *Book of the Duchess*", *Chaucer Review* 35: 281–93, at 281.

> Be oure Lord, hyt ys to deye soone.
> For nothyng I leve hyt noght,
> But lyve and deye ryght in this thoght;
> For there nys planete in firmament,
> Ne in ayr ne in erthe noon element,
> That they ne yive me a yifte echone
> Of wepynge whan I am alone.
> For whan that I avise me wel
> And bethenke me every del
> How that ther lyeth in rekenyng,
> In my sorwe, for nothyng,
> And how ther leveth no gladnesse
> May glade me of my distresse,
> And how I have lost suffisance,
> And therto I have no plesance,
> Than may I say I have ryght noght.
> And whan al this falleth in my thought,
> Allas, than am I overcome!
> For that ys doon ys not to come.
> I have more sorowe than Tantale." (683–709)

This passage makes it painfully clear that the Man in Black mourns a person, not a chess piece. Yet the narrator does not acknowledge this, or any of the other clues as they come forth in diminishing subtlety.

Conclusions

As far as we know, the *Book of the Duchess* was Chaucer's first original narrative; it is also unique in that it was centred upon a singular rhetorical purpose. In the reading above I have tried to outline how Chaucer endows his narrator with qualified, limited knowledge and analytical tools, which would have made him appear exceptionally out of touch with human experience and noble culture while at the same time allowing Chaucer the space to write an inoffensive, sensitive poem to help console England's second most powerful man as he mourned the death of his first wife.

Chaucer asserts that he has an impossible task before him, and does not try to do what is beyond his abilities. This is why the narrator (and thus Chaucer) fails at consoling the Black Knight (and thus Gaunt); but the shared experience of Chaucer's attempt brings him and Gaunt together in a community of shared misery and interdependence, while the narrator's deference to Gaunt ensures that this is not misconstrued as an inappropriate attempt at socially disruptive egalitarianism. While the narrator stylistically functions in the poem as the frame for the Man in Black's complaint, this same narrator rhetorically functions in the real world to negotiate an appropriate relationship between John of Gaunt and Chaucer, whereby the former will forgive the latter if he ever seems too obtuse or offensive. The narrator elevates the Man in Black by appearing callous while the knight is courtly; in an allegorical conflation of the character and the person, John of Gaunt appears a man of exceptional grace and nobility. The narrator, on the other hand, is from beginning to end an outsider to the world of courtly love and genteel discourse. He is at times rude because he is obtuse, and he is almost always socially inept because he is not privy to the ennobling emotions of fine loving. Chaucer's audience is invited to see these characteristics in the poet himself, while the poem betrays his own tender sensitivity in the most subtle ways while explicitly suggesting a daft, rustic non-courtliness.

The task of consoling a grieving person is never a light burden. For Chaucer, this burden was made worse by the precarious and awkward social position the situation provided him. There seems to be little reason to understand Chaucer's representations of himself and Gaunt in this poem as anything other than an act of social deference to a man of considerable power and a political gesture to proclaim (or, depending on how we date the poem, to confirm) an alliance. The narrator in the dream maintains an inferior position, characterised by gaucheness, in order to allow Chaucer to affirm his inferior position to John of Gaunt in the real world of the poem's initial reception. If Chaucer's audience is invited to conflate the narrator with the poet himself, then he is inviting his contemporaries to see him as an awkward, hat-holding clerk outside the world of courtly love and, as is made abundantly clear, unable to understand it or its language no matter how explicit the case is made. When we consider the poem in its historical context, the reason for these characterisations becomes obvious: Chaucer wrote a poem with a keen sensitivity to Gaunt's suffering for all to hear in order to affirm his allegiance to the nobleman, while appearing inferior to the courtly world he is at pains to represent. The narrator is removed so far from human life as experienced by members of the nobility that he and Chaucer cannot possibly seem to be overstepping their boundaries. At the same time, the Man in Black's soulful expression reaffirms the pain of Gaunt's loss, and offers a poetic expression of his misery.

Chapter 3
The Scholar of Love: The Dream Visions

Asocial Reading Habits in the Dream Visions

I have already examined how the narrator's reading of the romance book at the beginning of *Book of the Duchess* serves to frame his character and the poem in general; here I would like to extend my observations to Chaucer's later dream visions. For the most part, the narrator's reading habits characterise him as an author-creator. This has already been suggested by Joyce Coleman, who observes that Chaucer uses "read" more often than "hear" to describe his or his narrator's reading habits, and that his uses of this word "invoke the specialised form of reading characteristic of authors or of scholars" which Coleman calls "literary- and scholarly-professional reading".[1] This representation of the narrator often foregrounds his agency as a transmitter of old texts for a new audience; thus his reading is often part of his responsibilities as a poet.[2] As a result, "Chaucer-the-character's private lust for reading is transmuted through dream and imagination into material of broad social benefit – hygienic, educational, and historical".[3]

Joyce Coleman suggests that this is a consistent characterisation of a "fictional persona"[4] that depends upon his audience's presupposed knowledge of Chaucer as a poet – even in a text as early as *Book of the Duchess*.[5] Here I would like to relate Coleman's observations about this fictionalised persona to Chaucer himself outside the

[1] *Public Reading and the Reading Public in Late Medieval England and France*. Cambridge: Cambridge University Press, 1996: 153.
[2] Ibid., 169–77.
[3] Ibid., 177.
[4] Ibid., 175.
[5] Ibid., 174.

text by continuing my study of the narrator as a rhetorical self-representation. From such a perspective, the characterisation of the narrator's reading habits is meant to inform the audience's understanding of the author's habits of reading and writing.

I also hope to extend Coleman's analysis of the narrator's reading habits to show a development in Chaucer's self-representation; not only do the narrator's reading habits characterise Chaucer as a maker of poetry, but his reading is often inexact and inept, suggesting that a more public way of reading is to be preferred and that books, ultimately, are merely the representations of their authors' voices, best debated openly amongst a community of readers. Larry Sklute sees the narrator's reading habits as a central aspect of Chaucer's self-representation: "Chaucer's persona [i.e. the narrators of his works] is essentially a bookish personality, less comfortable even in dreams with grand flights above the earth than with sitting in the study reading".[6] This description, Sklute opines, is appropriate for all of Chaucer's narrators, and I believe that the texts often support this interpretation, which I will here extend to the context of social, public reading that was the norm for Chaucer's contemporaries.

Chaucer's references to his textual sources bring to his audience's mind the image of Chaucer pouring over books alone to compile the English poetry he eventually offers. In one of his earliest texts, *Anelida and Arcite*, he tells his audience that he found "this olde storie, in Latyn" (10). *Troilus and Criseyde* is also the product of the narrator's bookish knowledge; the Latinate "Lollius" is always his only source for the story of Troilus, and the narrator constantly proclaims that his knowledge of the story is limited by what he has read, so he cannot tell his audience if Criseyde had any children: "I rede it naught, therefore I late it goon" (I.133). Elsewhere, the relationship between his reading and his writing is less directly outlined. In the *Book of the Duchess*, the narrator informs his audience that he would read romances to "drive the night away" (49) as he lies sleepless in bed (36–7). In the *Parliament of Fowls*, the narrator says that he knows of Love only from books, and not from real experience:

6 *Virtue of Necessity: Inconclusiveness and Narrative Form in Chaucer's Poetry.* Columbus, Ohio: Ohio State University Press, 1984: 23.

> For al be that I knowe nat Love in dede,
> Ne wot how that he quiteth folk here hyre,
> Yit happeth me ful ofte in bokes reede
> Of his myrakles and his crewel yre. (8–11)

In the following stanza, Chaucer emphasises the narrator's bookishness with a rather redundant description of his reading habits:

> Of usage – what for lust and what for lore –
> On bokes rede I ofte, as I yow tolde.
> But wherfore that I speke al this? Nat yoore
> Agon it happede me for to beholde
> Upon a bok, was write with letters olde,
> And therupon, a certeyn thing to lerne,
> The longe day ful faste I redde and yerne. (15–21)

Most of the space in *Parliament of Fowls* is devoted to presenting the various voices of the birds as they debate which of the three tercel eagles deserves the love of the formel. The debate is unfruitful, and Nature finally decides that the formel should choose her mate for herself. Unable to make a decision, the bird asks for another year to decide, and the poem ends without resolution.

The narrator, however, is not satisfied with waiting, and hopes to find the resolution for the birds' inconclusive debate in books:

> I wok, and othere bokes tok me to,
> To reede upon, and yit I rede alwey.
> I hope, ywis, to rede so som day
> That I shal mete som thyng for to fare
> The bet, and thus to rede I nyl nat spare. (693–9)

With these words, Chaucer leaves his audience with the lingering image of him returning to his library to search, like a scholar of love, for the information he needs. In this fashion he begins and ends *Parliament of Fowls* as a reader who yearns to glean "al this newe science that men lere" from books (25). For him, that science includes love poetry, a form of public entertainment for his intended audience, who are invited to debate the virtues of the three birds, and to mediate the decision that Nature (and, of course, Chaucer) does not provide.

By leaving the decision unmade, Chaucer refuses to take the role that the cuckoo offers for himself:

> "And I for worm-foul," seyde the fol kokkow,
> "For I wol of myn owene autorite,
> For comune spede, take on the charge now,
> For to delyvere us is gret charite." (505–8)

Throughout Chaucer's poetry one gets the sense that the common profit is best served through an open debate, in which books themselves play a small part (we will see this theme most clearly in *Troilus and Criseyde* and the *Tale of Melibee*). In the *Parliament*, Chaucer opens the debate and implicitly chides anyone who would close the discussion by proclaiming his or her autonomous right to the truth, while overtly distancing himself from the debate by hiding behind books. The narrator suggests this is a noble search when he tells his audience that

> For out of olde feldes, as men seyth,
> Cometh al this newe corn from yer to yere,
> And out of olde bokes, in good feyth,
> Cometh al this newe science that men lere.
> But now to purpos as of this matere:
> To rede forth hit gan me so delite
> That al that day me thoughte but a lyte. (22–8)

This is a common sentiment of the Middle Ages: in old books truth can be found. Yet as noble as the search for truth in these old books might be, the narrator's reading offers no answers. As a result, his audience is invited to debate the issue and come to their own resolution. The authority that Chaucer's position as an author and reader might provide him is sublimated, while his audience is given ultimate control over the text's resolution by inviting them to answer the questions he cannot.

The *Parliament of Fowls* begins and ends with an image of the narrator as a lonely reader and writer,[7] while his relationship to the

---

[7] See James Wilhelm, "The Narrator and His Narrative in Chaucer's *Parlement*", *Chaucer Review* 1 (1967): 201–6, for a reading of this poem that has largely in-

figure of the lover is analogous but ultimately disparate.[8] Robert O. Payne makes a similar case for all of Chaucer's narrators, suggesting that they progressively become more integral to the text in the dream visions, and that this development culminates in the *Prologue* to the *Legend of Good Women*, where the narrator is portrayed as a writer on a quest for an *ars poetica*.[9] Although I believe the narrator is integral to the *Book of the Duchess*, Payne's observation nevertheless uncovers Chaucer's growing fascination with representing his agency in the process of transforming old texts into new, and with the question of texts' relationship to the real world they serve. In essence, the narrator's development from the *Book of the Duchess* to the *Legend of Good Women* is that of the social outsider who increasingly becomes concerned with his own representation of society, while seeming to maintain his distance.

Although the narrator is motivated to read because he wants to learn more about humanity, his textual proclivities more often distance him from his ultimate goal, and he appears, as a result, separate from the worlds he describes and inhabits. Many scholars have been struck by the emotional detachment of Chaucer's narrators (except, interestingly, in *Troilus and Criseyde*, which I discuss in Chapter 4), although this varies in degree from poem to poem.

For example, the narrator of the *Parliament of Fowls* appears more emotionally detached than the dreamer of the *Book of the Duchess*.[10] An understanding of *Book of the Duchess* as a socially moti-

fluenced the discussion that follows. While Wilhelm sees the narrator as a frame for the discussion of love that is central to the poem, he does not engage the issue of Chaucer's relationship to the narrator as a social persona.

8   For a discussion of the parallel characterisation of the narrator, see Marion Polzella, "'The Craft So Long to Lerne': Poet and Lover in Chaucer's *Envoy to Scogan* and *Parliament of Fowls*", *Chaucer Review* 10 (1976): 279–86.

9   "Making His Own Myth: The *Prologue* to Chaucer's *Legend of Good Women*", *Chaucer Review* 9 (1975): 197–211. Sheila Delany makes a similar argument for the *Legend of Good Women* as a whole, which, she suggests, is preoccupied with the reception of Chaucer's texts (see *The Naked Text: Chaucer's* Legend of Good Women. Berkeley, Calif.: University of California Press, 1994, esp. Chs. 1 and 5).

10 Kathleen E. Dubs and Stoddard Malarkey, "The Frame of Chaucer's *Parlement*", *Chaucer Review* 13 (1978): 16–24.

vated rhetorical text uncovers the reason for this difference in character. The *Parliament of Fowls* does not have the consolatory function of *Book of the Duchess* and it was not written, as far as we know, for a single man enduring a great tragedy.

The poem gives few clues as to its date of composition or the event of its reception. Henry Kelly has suggested that its setting is the day of St. Valentine of Genoa (3 May), and that the Valentine's Day of the poem is a reference to the tradition surrounding this particular Valentine.[11] This explains the spring imagery of the poem and would suggest that the poem was written for a spring performance under less tragic circumstances than those of *Book of the Duchess*.

This context allowed Chaucer to present various perspectives on love in a comic debate that could then be continued amongst his audience members, who could mediate the meaning his text does not provide. Piero Boitani has argued that at the centre of the *Parliament* is "love directed towards the *bonum commune*",[12] while David Aers suggests that Chaucer overcomes difficulties in the notion of common profit in the *Parliament of Fowls* by relying upon authoritative interpretation, which in turn becomes a method of resolving social conflict.[13] Whether this is indeed Chaucer's or the narrator's ideal is a question beyond my present scope, except to say in general terms that the connection between textual communication and social interaction in the real world is clearly central to the narrator's characterisation in the poem. This is how Chaucer rhetorically constructs his position vis-à-vis the poem's undefined and unresolved conclusion.

Contra Aers, James Dean argues that the structure of the poem itself undermines any sense of conclusion that can be got from it; thus the dreamer's awakening hints that the questions presented in the poem

---

11 "The Genoese Saint and Chaucer's Third of May", *Chaucer Newsletter* 1 (1979): 6–10. See also Kelly's *Chaucer and the Cult of St Valentine*. Leiden: Brill, 1986 for a more sustained study.

12 "Old Books Brought to Life in Dreams: The *Book of the Duchess*, the *House of Fame* and the *Parliament of Fowls*", in *The Cambridge Chaucer Companion*, Piero Boitani and Jill Mann (eds.). Cambridge: Cambridge University Press, 1986: 39–57.

13 "The *Parliament of Fowls*: Authority, the Knower and the Known", *Chaucer Review* 16 (1981): 1–17.

might never be resolved.[14] Larry Sklute similarly argues that the *Parliament of Fowls* leaves its audience unsatisfied and its questions unanswered so as to suggest that in reality there is no one true answer – only a multitude of voices.[15] Whatever Chaucer's thematic intent in the poem, these readings share an understanding of the narrator as a man of books who relies upon them for knowledge of the world, and yet who fails to provide answers, much like the poem itself. Audience members are consequently forced to come to their own conclusion through a process of communal mediation.

If, as David Aers claims, Chaucer argues in the *Parliament of Fowls* for a unification of viewpoints by recourse to textual authority, the *House of Fame* is about the failings of textual authority. The narrator of this poem is named Geffrey, and, like Chaucer, he is a comptroller of customs. He is more bookish than the narrators of the other short dream visions, and he is chastised for being removed from the real world by his tireless reading:

> And noght oonly fro fer contree
> That ther no tydynge cometh to thee,
> But of thy verray neyghebores,
> That duellen almost at thy dores,
> Thou herist neyther that ne this;
> For when thy labour doon al ys,
> And hast mad alle thy rekenynges,
> In stede of reste and newe thynges
> Thou goost hom to thy hous anoon,
> And, also domb as any stoon,
> Thou sittest at another book
> Tyl fully daswed ys thy look;
> And lyvest thus as an heremyte,
> Although thyn abstinence ys lyte. (647–61)

We could come to Geffrey's defence by arguing that the speaker of this passage, the Eagle who guides the narrator to the House of Fame

---

14 "Artistic Conclusiveness in Chaucer's *Parliament of Fowls*", *Chaucer Review* 21 (1986): 16–25.
15 "The Inconclusive Form of the *Parliament of Fowls*", *Chaucer Review* 16 (1981): 119–28.

as a reward for his tireless work for Love, is not trustworthy. Yet in no way does the Eagle prove to be unreliable at any moment. His authority is first implied by his station as a servant of Jupiter who can, and does, send Geffrey to the House of Fame, and his reliability is reinforced by his knowledge of the real world, such as the true nature of the heavens. Also, Geffrey's apathy to real world experience later in the poem supports the Eagle's admonishments, and his preference for his books suggests that they are the narrator's – and, we are invited to assume, Chaucer's – only connection to human experience.

Strikingly at odds with Geffrey's private and silent reading habits was the public reading of fourteenth century readers. For Geffrey, reading is not a communal activity; in fact, as the Eagle tells us, it excludes him from society by keeping his attention from the tidings of his neighbours. Here Chaucer seems to be taking advantage of the typical mode of textual transmission in his era to distance his narrator from society; because Geffrey, unlike his audience, reads texts silently and alone, he becomes a stranger to his neighbours, lost in a world of books without any knowledge of the real world.

The narrator's devotion to his books might be admirable if he learned something from them, yet Chaucer begins the *House of Fame* with the suggestion that he has, to use Stephen Kruger's phrase, a "confused ignorance"[16] of the nature of dreams:

> God turne us every drem to goode!
> For hyt is wonder, be the roode,
> To my wyt, what causeth swevenes
> Eyther on morwes or on evenes,
> And why th'effect folweth of somme,
> And of somme hit shal never come;
> Why that is in avision
> And why this a revelacion,
> Why this a drem, why that a sweven,
> And noght to every man lyche even;
> Why this a fantome, why these oracles,
> I not; but whoso of these miracles
> The causes knoweth bet then I,

16 *Dreaming in the Middle Ages.* Cambridge: Cambridge University Press, 1992: 57.

> Devyne he, for I certainly
> Ne kan hem noght, ne never thinke
> To besily my wyt to swinke
> To knowe of hir signifiaunce
> The gendres, neyther the distaunce
> Of tymes of hem, ne the causes,
> Or why this more then that cause is –
> As yf folkys complexions
> Make hem dreme of reflexions,
> Or ellys thus, as other sayn,
> For to gret feblenesse of her brayn,
> By absinence or by seknesse,
> Prison-stewe or gret distresse,
> Or ellys by dysordynaunce
> Of naturel acustumaunce,
> That som man is to curious
> In studye, or melancolyous,
> Or thus so inly ful of drede
> That no man may hym bote bede. (I.1–32)

I will not quote further, but it is worth mentioning that Chaucer continues to present alternatives for another twenty lines. Here Chaucer employs *occupatio* to overwhelm the audience with a complex exposition of dream theory and its terminology, even though he never organises his knowledge into wisdom. He ends this catalogue of possible causes of dreams by simply saying: "But why the cause is, noght wot I" (I.52). In this singular dismissal Kruger finds a refusal on the narrator's part "to organize dream lore into any coherent system" and a refusal "to become a theorist".[17]

The narrator's ignorance is not necessarily betrayed by this passage, since his professed ignorance is not of medieval dream theory, but rather of the truth of the matter. It might be that this passage is meant to affirm his knowledge of the dream-theory tradition but not of the reality of dreams. Thus his reading has been in vain, and we can conclude that this is either due to the limitations of human knowledge in general, or because Geffrey personally is too obtuse to root through the complex theories before him.

---

17   Ibid.

Jacqueline Miller has suggested that the narrator of the *House of Fame* rejects both the dream-vision tradition and textual authority altogether.[18] In her reading, the narrator

> at different intervals...tries out different ways of removing himself from the need to confront all this confusing material [i.e. authoritative texts] by handing over the problem – and the possibility of resolution – to others: leaving the "grete clerkys" to work it out (53–4); in fact, letting *anyone* who can determine these things do so.[19]

This is certainly the case in his retelling of the Dido myth, where the narrator – and, it seems, Chaucer – boldly and unapologetically proclaim the superiority of this interpretation to that of Virgil, one of the most revered Latin authors, although his rhetorical method of making the same point is the exact opposite of what we find at the beginning of the poem. After telling us that Aeneas "betrayed" Dido and "lefte hir ful unkyndely" (294), the narrator recounts her complaint and bluntly tells his audience in a direct address:

> In suche wordes gan to pleyne
> Dydo of hir grete peyne,
> As me mette redely –
> Non other auctour alegge I. (311–14)

For an English vernacular author of the late fourteenth century, such a statement is daring. Here Chaucer rejects Virgil's account of Aeneas' abandonment of Dido because his own fictional eyewitness account makes him a greater authority: his firsthand experience transcends the rumours offered in the *Aeneid*.

This unprecedented rhetorical gesture was unnecessary; Chaucer could have referred to the authority of Book VII of *Heroides*, where Ovid defends Dido and accuses Aeneas of abandoning her. While their similar accounts reflect Chaucer's debt to Ovid and perhaps their

---

18 "The Writing on the Wall: Authority and Authorship in Chaucer's *House of Fame*", *Chaucer Review* 17 (1982): 95–115.
19 Ibid., 103.

shared temperament,[20] Chaucer chooses his own authority over Ovid's to defend Dido from Virgil's slander. While his adaptation of Ovid fits Helen Cooper's observation that "Chaucer's Ovid is curiously modern in comparison with the moralised Ovids so prevalent in his century",[21] he chooses to silence the Latin poet while defending Dido not within an ancient literary tradition that is reliable and authoritative, but with recourse to his unique individual experience.

Laurel Amtower suggests that this is one moment where Chaucer advocates an ethics of reading in the *House of Fame*, and that the narrator's reading of Dido is an example of a correct moral judgment, here expressed with confidence.[22] But it is not a bookish reading, and between this explicit moral judgment and the narrator's professed reliance on books elsewhere we find the gap between Chaucer's self-representation as a bookworm and his actual concern with the failings of the books others have relied on. These do not reveal a fallible or inconsistent narrator, but a slip of Chaucer's rhetorical mask as he moves the focus away from his own position in society and literary tradition to the plight of Dido and, presumably, to the cause of women in general while engaging issues of "a poet's alternative resources; namely, the resources of preexisting story, or the resources provided by his own empirical experience".[23]

The narrator's sympathy for Dido is unusual for two reasons: it is an affirmation of his personal authority and a rejection of textual cul-

---

20 "Chaucer's conception of the character and spirit of Dido had evidently already been formed from the *Heroides*" (Edgar Finley Shannon, *Chaucer and the Roman Poets*. Cambridge, Mass.: Harvard University Press, 1929: 59). See also John Fyler, *Chaucer and Ovid*. New Haven, Conn.: Yale University Press, 1979 and Michael Calabrese, *Chaucer's Ovidian Arts of Love*. Gainesville, Fl.: University of Florida Press, 1994: esp. 11–32, who provide studies of the Ovidian/Chaucerian temperament vis-à-vis the Virgilian/Dantean.
21 Helen Cooper, "Chaucer and Ovid: A Question of Authority" in *Ovid Renewed: Ovidian Influences on Literature and Art from the Middle Ages to the Twentieth Century*, Charles Martindale (ed.). Cambridge: Cambridge University Press, 1988: 71–88, at 74.
22 "Authorizing the Reader in Chaucer's *House of Fame*", *Philological Quarterly* 79 (2000): 273–91.
23 Alcuin Blamires, "A Chaucer Manifesto", *Chaucer Review* 24 (1989): 29–43, at 30–1.

ture. The narrator much more commonly shows an over-reliance on texts for knowledge. His bookishness becomes the backdrop for another scene in the *House of Fame* that rhetorically complements the Dido-scene's *ethos* while contradicting it on the level of stylistic characterisation. On his journey to the heavens to see the stars first-hand, the narrator is rather indifferent, although we might expect him to be eager to learn:

> "Lat be," quod he [the Eagle], "thy fantasye!
> Wilt thou lere of sterres aught?"
> "Nay, certeynly," quod y, "right naught."
> "And why?" "For y am now to old."
> "Elles I wolde the have told,"
> Quod he, "the sterres names, lo,
> And al the hevenes sygnes therto,
> And which they ben." "No fors," quod y.
> "Yis, pardee," quod he; "wostow why?
> For when thou redest poetrie,
> How goddes gonne stellifye
> Bridd, fissh, best, or him or here,
> As the Raven or eyther Bere,
> Or Arionis harpe fyn,
> Castor, Pollux, or Delphyn,
> Or Athalantes doughtres sevene,
> How alle these arn set in hevene;
> For though thou have hem ofte on honde,
> Yet nostow not wher that they stonde."
> "No fors," quod y, "hyt is no need.
> I leve as wel, so God me spede,
> Hem that write of this matere,
> As though I knew her places here." (II.992–1014)

Geffrey's listless reaction would be striking in our own era; at a time when the skies were a much greater mystery, his apathy is absurd. As Bertrand H. Bronson notes, Chaucer's

> contemporaries more frequently raised their eyes to the heavens than lowered them to the earth. The continual references in his work to the movements and

positions of the heavenly bodies far outweigh his allusions to the natural scene as of significance to men's lives.[24]

Despite popular and academic interest in the stars and their significance, Geffrey simply does not care to see them firsthand, choosing instead to read at home, alone. Again, his professed reliance on books characterises him as a literary-professional outside the real world of experience and human interaction.

If we examine the narrator's independent proclamation of Dido's suffering as a characterisation of the narrator as an autonomous fiction, it seems to be in blatant contradiction to the narrator's later apathy to first-hand experience. But if we compare these moments as different rhetorical gestures, they become complimentary. At one point Chaucer can demonstrate the failure of texts by showing how they can depict an innocent woman and victim of treachery as the instigator, while at another he can depict himself as an example of the foolishness of an over-reliance on texts. Although contradictory from a modern stylistic perspective, these characterisations are complementary rhetorical gestures that, on the whole, emphasise the *ethos* of the *House of Fame*: the perspectives of individuals are inherently flawed and subservient to a "gret auctorite" (III.2158) beyond the scope of any one person.

Unfortunately, Chaucer never provides this great authority – he stopped writing the *House of Fame* just before "the man of gret auctorite" could soothe the cacophony of the individual voices of fame and rumour with the definitive word of truth. Chaucer's refusal to give this authority, for whatever reason, is analogous to the structures of his dream visions, which typically lack thematic closure and fail to pronounce judgment on the problems they engage. The *Book of the Duchess* ends with the deflation of the Black Knight's courtly discourse, and he does not receive the consolation he needs and is promised. In the *Parliament of Fowls*, the narrator is rewarded for his asocial, scholarly toil for Love with a dream vision that provides no answers, and ends before we learn the formel's choice and the identity of that "certeyn thing" which the narrator seeks. Chaucer's narrative

---

24   *In Search of Chaucer*. Toronto: University of Toronto Press, 1960: 16.

strategy in these texts is to introduce an inquisitive narrator who finds a multitude of voices that provide no answers, much like the various voices in the Houses of Fame and Rumour. In the dream visions, Chaucer consistently refuses to give a possible solution to the great problems of courtly love or, in the case of the *House of Fame*, of worldly reputation, opting instead to retreat to the safer ground of ambiguity and an apparent dependence upon authority, while, in reality, he opens the question for public mediation, discussion and debate.

This state of affairs does not seem to bother the narrator, who appears to be removed from or afraid of real-world experience. Just as Geffrey complains that the stars

> shynen here so bryghte,
> Hyt shulde shenden al my syghte
> To loke on hem (II.1015–7)

so too the gaze of the narrator in the *Canterbury Tales* is downcast:

> "What man artow?" quod he [Harry Bailey];
> "Thou lookest as thou woldest fynde an hare,
> For evere upon the ground I se thee stare.
> "Approche neer, and looke up murily.
> Now war yow, sires, and lat this man have place!
> He in the waast is shape as wel as I;
> This were a popet in an arm t'enbrace
> For any womman, smal and fair of face.
> He semeth elvyssh by his contenaunce,
> For unto no wight dooth he daliaunce." (VII.695–704)

The Host's coarseness aside, this description fits Geffrey of the *House of Fame* in almost every detail. In both texts the narrator looks neither at the people around him nor at the mysteries of the heavens; he is shy and removed. This was, of course, not the sort of man Chaucer was – the records and his poetic sensitivity tell a different story – but it is the sort of impression that Chaucer gives of himself, as an irrelevant, unworldly man, an outside observer who sees the world only through books and cannot make sense of the voices around him. Hence J. J. Anderson's observation that the narrators of the *Book of the Duchess* and the *House of Fame* "are comic symbols of futility, because, so it is implied, their one-sidedness [i.e., their over-dependence upon authority and not on experience] reduces them to impotence".[25] In this sense the narrator is a scholarly reader limited by his bibliophilic propensities, whether due to a failure of intelligence, a tact that stops him short, an insensitivity to human experience unsuccessfully remedied by reading, or any number of other alternatives. Chaucer's narrators are ambiguous enough to leave this question open to continual debate, much like the issue of appropriate consolation to a grieving man, or the right choice amongst the three eagles of *Parliament of Fowls*, or the voice of authority that will silence all rumour.

The last of Chaucer's dream visions, the *Prologue* to the *Legend of Good Women*, provides us with another scholarly narrator whose insensitivity is at focus. Here he expresses a reverence for books that becomes faith:

> Than mote we to bokes that we fynde,
> Thurgh whiche that olde thinges ben in mynde,
> And to the doctrine of these olde wyse,
> Yeve credence, in every skylful wise,
> That tellen of these olde appreved stories
> Of holynesse, of regnes, of victories,
> Of love, of hate, of other sondry thynges,
> Of whiche I may not maken rehersynges.
> And yf that olde bokes were aweye,
> Yloren were of remembraunce the keye.
> Wel ought us thanne honouren and beleve
> These bokes, there we han noon other preve. (F.17–28; cf. G.17–28)

Although it is no effort to imagine that Chaucer honoured books, his respect is never so unquestioning. His audience, however, is invited to imagine that his love for books is blind devotion, an implication reinforced in the following lines:

> On bokes for to rede I me delyte,
> And to hem yive I feyth and ful credence,
> And in myn herte have hem in reverence.

---

25 "The Narrators in the *Book of the Duchess* and the *Parlement of Fowls*", *Chaucer Review* 26 (1992): 219–35, at 220.

> So hertely, that ther is game noon
> That fro my bokes maketh me to goon (F.30–4; cf. G.30–4)

Elsewhere in the *Prologue*, Chaucer suggests that "men shulde autoritees beleve,/There as there lyth non other assay by preve" (G.83–4, cf. F.99–100), and faith in the tradition of canonicity and canonisation is sufficient to determine who is and who is not an authority. Yet the lingering implication is that these canons are created and mediated by human beings, who themselves are ultimately and unavoidably fallible.

Alceste rebukes such blind faith in a line unique to the later G-version: "Al ne is nat gospel that is to yow pleyned" (G.326).[26] The mediation of truth in texts invites textual discourse to continue, and allows the God of Love to order the narrator to write the *Legend of Good Women* as recompense for his transgressions. In the F-version, the God of Love encourages the narrator to use texts ("in thy bookes alle thou shalt hem fynde", F. 556) and to "reherce of al hir lyf the grete,/After thise olde auctours lysten for to trete" (F.574–5). This textual focus diminishes in the G-version, where the God of Love simply tells him to write the stories of virtuous ladies after he asks with exasperation: "Hast thow nat in a bok, lyth in thy cheste,/The grete gooodnesse of the queene Alceste?" (G.499–500, cf. F.510–11). Chaucer's progression away from books towards the real world, made manifest in the *Canterbury Tales*, is found in this shift away from presenting his poem as a voice among a world of texts.

The narrator, however, remains characterised by his relationship to texts and textuality in both versions of the *Prologue* to the *Legend of Good Women* (for more on this aspect of the narrator, see Chapter 5). Although the narrator's devotion to his books wanes in the month

---

26 Currently there is a general consensus that the F-version predates the G-version; since lines F.496–7 most likely refer to Queen Anne, who arrived in England in early 1382 and died in June 1394, the F-version was most likely written during this period. The G-version omits these two lines, suggesting that it was written after 1394. John Fisher argues that the G-version was written to commemorate Richard's marriage to Isabella of France, who was crowned in London on 7 January 1397 – see "The Revision of the *Prologue* to the *Legend of Good Women*: An Occasional Explanation", *South Atlantic Bulletin* 43 (1978): 75–84.

of May, when "the foules synge,/And that the floures gynnen for to sprynge" (*LGW* F.37–8; cf. G.37–8), he is still a bookworm for the rest of the year, remaining as devoted to books as the narrators of Chaucer's earlier dream visions. It is thus no surprise that in the *Canterbury Tales* the narrator tells his fellow pilgrims: "oother tale certes kan I noon,/But of a rym I *lerned* longe agoon" (VII.708–9, italics added). As in the dream visions, the narrator here learns of romance, tidings, and love through books, while remaining removed from the real world of human interaction. In *Book of the Duchess* the narrator's scholarly ways are emphasised by his habit of reading alone in bed, in contrast to the couples of the poem and the implied lovers in his audience, not least of whom was John of Gaunt. In the *Parliament of Fowls* and the *House of Fame*, the narrator is explicitly characterised as a scholar of love who either hopes to learn of love by reading it (*PF* 693–9) or who stays at home serving the God of Love by reading instead of interacting with his neighbours (*HF* 649–68). The *Legend of Good Women* continues this characterisation, while Chaucer begins to remove his poetry from textual debate and into the real world of human comedy portrayed in the *Canterbury Tales*.

Social and Scholarly Reading in the *Canterbury Tales*

Chaucer imagined a character who shares his narrators' love of books and learning when he described the Clerk of the *Canterbury Tales*, that pilgrim to Canterbury who "[o]f studie took he moost cure and mooste heede" (I.303), and who owned twenty books "in blak or reed,/ Of Aristotle and his philosophie" (I.294–5). This was not a small collection (it is a third the size of the narrator's library in the *Legend of Good Women* – see G.273) when we consider the cost of books in the era and the Clerk's youth. The source for his tale is none other than an exotic foreign poet, whose talents are described in academic terms:

> Fraunceys Petrak, the lauriat poete,
> Highte this clerk, whos rethorike sweete

> Enlumyned al Ytaille of poetrie,
> As Lynyan dide of philosophie,
> Or lawe, or oother art particular. (IV.31–5)

Here Petrarch, an obscure Italian for Chaucer's audience, is characterised as a rhetorically adept clerk comparable to Giovanni da Lignano, an equally obscure Italian academic. By these references the Clerk's bookish sensibility and ambitious erudition are made sufficiently clear.

Like the Clerk, the dream-vision narrators read for edification, although their choice in texts differs wildly; while the Clerk reads exotic Italian texts and serious, scholarly philosophy, the narrator's scholarly attention is largely directed to the stories of love that delight and entertain his audience, making him as irreverent as the Clerk is learned. I have already suggested that Chaucer creates this self-identification by referring to himself through his narrator as a reader of love-poetry; here I would like to explore how the mode of his narrator's reading and his seeming inability to grasp what he reads contrasted with the typical reading methods of his contemporaries.

Books are the source-material for much of Chaucer's poetry and the variety of Chaucer's true sources is well beyond the limits of his explicit citations. Often his selectivity appears to have a rhetorical effect, and his particular attention to books of love frames his character as a love poet while distancing him from the game of love itself. At the same time, Chaucer's erudition on a variety of subjects is difficult to ignore, and the display of his learning so omnipresent in his works is mitigated by his admissions that he is unable to understand his texts (as in the *Parliament of Fowls* and the *Book of the Duchess*) and that he cannot relate his experience of texts to experience of the world (as in the *House of Fame*). On the surface his love for books does not appear to be met by a deep understanding of them, while a closer reading shows the obvious sophistication and sensitivity of his responses to the authors that preceded him.

The narrator's insensitivity is an obtuse misunderstanding and a gauche underestimation of the complexities of human nature. Part of his problem is that his reading is private. Unlike the nobility who read texts in the public sphere, in which the reception of the work became a social, inclusive act, the narrator is alone with his books, and lacks the opportunity (and perhaps the desire) to compare his responses to and understandings of texts with those of other readers, whereas the reality for Chaucer's audiences would have been precisely the contrary – texts are to be shared in a social, public forum. Chaucer, by contrast, appears a dim scholar of love entirely removed from the community of his contemporaries and their method of receiving texts.

An unfortunate example of the communal experience of literature and the excited debates it can create is enacted – quite possibly parodied – in the *Wife of Bath's Prologue*, where the Wife of Bath's fifth husband, Jankyn the clerk (III.595), reads aloud and purely for pleasure. Unlike the Clerk of the frame-tale, Jankyn is a "joly clerk" (III.628) who

> hadde a book that gladly, nyght and day,
> For his desport he wolde rede alway;
> He cleped it Valerie and Theofraste,
> At which book he lough alwey ful faste.
> …
> And every nyght and day was his custume,
> Whan he hadde leyser and vacacioun
> From oother worldly occupacioun,
> To reden on this book of wikked wyves. (III.669–89)

He reads his collection of misogynist stories for entertainment, and so he reads aloud, much to the Wife of Bath's disdain:

> Upon a nyght Jankyn, that was oure sire,
> Redde on his book, as he sat by the fire,
> Of Eva first, that for hir wikkednesse
> Was al mankynde broght to wrecchednesse,
> …
> Tho redde he me how Sampson loste his heres
> …
> Tho redde he me, if that I shal nat lyen,
> Of Hercules and of his Dianyre,
> …
> He tolde me eek for what occasioun
> Amphiorax at Thebes loste his lyf.
> …
> Of Lyvia tolde he me, and of Lucye
> …

> Thanne tolde he me how oon Latumyus
> Compleyned unto his felawe Arrius
> ...
> Of latter date, of wyves hath he red
> That somme han slayn hir housbondes in hir bed,
> ...
> "Bet is," quod he, "thyn habitacioun
> Be with a leon or a foul dragoun,
> Than with a womman usynge for to chyde.
> Bet is," quod he, "hye in the roof abyde,
> Than with an angry wyf doun in the hous."
> ...
> And whan I saugh he wolde nevere fyne
> To reden on this cursed book al nyght,
> Al sodeynly thre leves have I plyght
> Out of his book, right as he radde, and eke
> I with my fest so took hym on the cheke
> That in oure fyr he fil bakward adoun. (III.713–93)

The Wife of Bath freely uses the verbs "redde" and "telle" interchangeably (cf. ll.740, 747, 757), and in lines 721 and 724 she uses a prepositionless dative "me" with the verb "redde". This is markedly different discourse from the more explicit, precise adverbial phrase "as domb as a stoon" which Chaucer uses to describe Geffrey's asocial reading habits. The insertion of this qualifier in the *House of Fame* suggests that silent reading was unusual enough to need explication, and that the narrator's reading habits are markedly abnormal. The Wife of Bath is more casual in describing Jankyn's mode of textual reception, although she is dedicated to emphasising the fact that Jankyn chooses not to spare her from these offensive stories. Her rhetorical method of expressing this is not by commenting on his mode of reading, but by employing *amplificatio* of the antifeminist tales and by repeating parallel verbal constructions involving "read" or "tell" as the verb, "he" as the subject, and the dative "me". This rhetoric highlights the texts, not Jankyn's method of transmitting them; what the Wife of Bath laments is not his habit of reading aloud, which includes her in the discourse of the book, but the subject of his texts, which invalidates her perspective and opinion.

For Jankyn and the Wife of Bath, their shared experience of literature is disastrous because the *ethos* of the stories is too offensive for the Wife of Bath's disposition, resulting in her retaliation by destroying the text. Ralph Hanna suggests that the Wife of Bath cannot approach the book in the same way as Jankyn does, because he reads it while she listens to it through the filter of Jankyn's voice. That voice

> exposes and subverts its [the book's] primary function – its claim to invoke universal truth. For what Jankyn voices is the personality he finds in the book – that it in fact states only a human point of view, that of the audience who keep the book alive by reading it.[27]

The compilers of such collections of stories practised a sort of "self-effacing" approach to their task by studying (or claiming to study) the variety of available texts.[28] As a result, the collection should appear to be a work of scholarship that aims to make more accessible the wisdom of textual authorities to a group of readers. Jankyn's insertion of his own voice into the text by his act of prelection subverts this process, and the text's clerical voice is subsequently subverted by the Wife of Bath in her argument that authoritative texts are the voices of other human beings and thus fallible. Hence her attitude toward these literary men is dismissive:

> Men may devyne and glosen, up and doun,
> But wel I woot, expres, withoute lye,
> God bad us for to wexe and multiplye;
> That gentil text kan I wel understonde. (III.26–9)

The fallibility of individual human voices implicit within Jankyn's book, and made manifest in his recitation, is to the Wife of Bath a point of open and fair contention, decidable by recourse to the only authority that matters – that of God.

---

27 *Pursuing History: Middle English Manuscripts and Their Texts*. Stanford: Stanford University Press, 1996: 252.
28 Ibid., 250. On the compiler's methods, see A. J. Minnis, *Medieval Theory of Authorship*. London: Scolar Press, 1988: 190–210.

If Jankyn reads his book aloud to the Wife of Bath to control or subvert her female voice, we can tentatively say that Jankyn approaches this act of public reading with the hope of subverting the Wife of Bath's perspective as a woman. Yet I think there is more to Jankyn's habit of vocalised reading, and that he reads the text aloud not only for the Wife of Bath's benefit but for his own pleasure. In light of medieval theories of textual representation of the voice, his choice to read aloud makes perfect sense. Augustine of Hippo conceived of letters as invented signs that refer to words, which are in turn sprung from thought:

> Necesse est enim cum uerum loquimur, id est quod scimus loquimur, ex ipsa scientia quam memoria tenemus nascatur uerbum est quod in corde dicimus, quod nec graecum est nec latinum nec linguae alicuius alterius, sed cum id opus est in eorum quibus loquimur perferre notitiam aliquod signum quo significetur assumitur. Et plerumque sonus, aliquando etiam nutus, ille aruibus, ille oculis exhibetur ut per signa corporalia etiam corporis sensibus uerbum quod mente gerimus innotescat. ... Sed haec atque huiusmodi signa corporalia suie auribus siue oculis praesentibus quibus loquimur exhibemus. Inuentae sunt etiam litterae per quas possemus et cum absentibus conloqui, sed ista signa sunt uocum, cum ipsae uoces in sermone nostro earum quas cogitamus signa sint rerum.

> For when we speak the truth, that is, speak of what we know, then the word which is born from the knowledge itself which we retain in the memory must be altogether of the same kind as that knowledge from which it is born. For the thought formed from that thing which we know is the word which we speak in our heart, and it is neither Greek, nor Latin, nor of any other language, but when we have to bring it to the knowledge of those to whom we are speaking, then some sign is assumed by which it may be made known. And generally this is a sound, but at times also a nod; the former is shown to the ears, the latter to the eyes, in order that that word which we bear in our mind may also become known by bodily signs to the senses of the body. ... But we make use of these and other corporeal signs of this kind when we speak to the eyes or the ears of those who are present. But letters have also been invented by which we can also speak to those who are absent; but the letters are the signs of words, while the

words themselves in our speech are signs of the things of which we are thinking.[29]

Letters, then, are a reflection of the voice, which is itself a reflection of thought; they are signs for the audible speech of the author who employs them. A similar argument can be found in the *Etymologiae* of Isidore of Seville, who posits that text is speech fixed and entrapped within a code of letters: "Litterae autem sunt indices rerum, signa verborum, quibus tanta vis est, ut nobis dicta absentium sine voce loquantur", "Letters are the indications of things, the signs of words, which have such a force that they, without sound, can tell us things which have been said by those absent".[30]

In this scheme, the sounds of the author have been trapped in the form of letters on a page, which become voiced again only by reading the text: "Litterae autem dictae quasi legiterae, quod iter legentibus praestent, vel quod in legendo iterentur", "And letters get their name from *legiterae*, because they show the way for readers; in other words, because they are repeated in reading".[31] When medieval thinkers explained the relationship between thought and its linguistic expression, they conceived of a chain of order from thought itself to its textual representation; according to Boethius,

> igitur haec sint quattuor: res, intellectus, vox, littera, rem concipit intellectus, intellectum vero voces designant, ipsas vero voces litterae significant.
>
> there are thus four things: the thing, intellect, the voice, the letter; the intellect conceives of the thing, the intellect truly designates a voice to the thing, and then letters signify the voice.[32]

---

29   *De Trinitate*, XV.10, translated by Stephen McKenna in St Augustine, *On the Trinity Books 8–15*, Gareth B. Matthews (ed.). Cambridge: Cambridge University Press, 2002, 180–1.
30   *Etymologiae* 1.3.1–2 (I am using W. M. Lindsay's edition, published by Oxford University Press in 1911).
31   Ibid.
32   *Commentarium in Librum Aristotelis Peri Hermeneias, Prima Editio* 1:37, quoted in Martin Irvine, "Medieval Grammatical Theory and Chaucer's *House of Fame*", *Speculum* 60 (1985): 850–76, at 856n.17.

Thus the transmission of thought to text requires the use of the voice, of which letters are a mere reflection. When Jankyn reads aloud, he releases not just the sense of the work but the *voice* of the author's words as well. From the Wife of Bath's perspective, however, it is not the author's voice which Jankyn educes from the text by his performance, but his own voice – which, when directed to the Wife of Bath, appears to her to be an imposition of what Hanna calls the voice of "clericalism".[33] The *Prologue* to the *Wife of Bath's Tale* becomes her attempt to subvert this oppressive voice by asserting her own. It is not surprising the Friar is the one to complain that the Wife of Bath tells "a long preamble of a tale" (III.831).

The narrator is another representation of clerkish devotion to the voices of texts, and he reads, whether on love, dreams, or history, for instruction. But he is not a serious scholar. He chooses love stories and romances, and never refers to the Aristotelian textbooks and obscure Italian poetry and legal discourse on the Clerk's bedside table. Even the *Dream of Scipio*, which the narrator reads in the *Parliament of Fowls*, can be understood as preparatory material for the writing of dream visions.

He also does not share Jankyn's delight in the voices of texts' authors. This is not to say that the narrator does not enjoy reading – he obviously does. But his enjoyment is in reading the matter of the text, and not its voice. At first glance, this might be surprising, and might lead us to assume that the narrator is a fictional character; but if we consider the narrator as a persona serving to shape an audience's perception of the author, the narrator's insensitivity to language is Chaucer's way of masking his agency in producing a new literary vernacular. Christopher Cannon observes that the

> careful reader may search but will search in vain for lines in which Chaucer *says* that he "invented" English literary language, but that same reader will be equally likely to come away from Chaucer's texts with the impression that he has claimed precisely this.[34]

---

33   *Pursuing History*, 252.
34   *The Making of Chaucer's English*. Cambridge: Cambridge University Press, 1998: 136.

Chaucer's narrative voice is a primary *locus* for hiding his literary and linguistic agency. As a result, he appears to be a parody of the astute intellectual who reads silently and alone for edification.

Unlike Jankyn, the narrator is not a jolly clerk, and he does not "songes make and wel endite,/Juste and eek daunce, and weel purtreye and write" like the Squire (I.95–6). His scholarly attitude towards poetry and love, as things to be grasped by meticulous study, is at once uncourtly and a parody of the true academic, such as philosophical Strode or a nominalist such as John Duns Scotus or a church reformer like John Wycliffe. The narrator is a poor reader from hermeneutic and aesthetic perspectives because he does not delight in the mode of expression and he never seems to grasp the meaning of what he reads. He is a literary and scholastic incompetent, and, when the text's audience conflates narrator and poet, Chaucer appears to share these failings. Outside the world of love, a dim reader, he can provide no answers to the questions of the world he writes for and is fascinated by, and he consistently removes himself from the debate while framing its questions for his audience to answer. In the end, Chaucer suggests, his recourse is to a life of meticulous study of love and poetry, alone, silent, and outside the realm of love. The absurdity of this implication is compounded by the fact that, for Chaucer's primary audience, his poetry is not to be studied – it is to be read and enjoyed much as Jankyn would do: as entertainment, boisterously and aloud.

Chapter 4
The Servant of Servants: *Troilus and Criseyde*

Troilus and Criseyde and Rhetorical Narrative

For many reasons, *Troilus and Criseyde* welcomes modern literary analysis. It is a completed narrative with a focus on its main characters; their psychological individuality, personal motivations, and relationships to the plot are described in greater detail than we find in many other Chaucerians texts, such as the *Knight's Tale*. Thus debate can continue on whether Troilus is innocent,[1] whether he is an effeminate lover,[2] or whether he indulges in the sin of sloth.[3] Yet such debates must be careful. The conception of a story as a narrative with a beginning, middle, and end involving characters that demand empathy and in some way develop is, although compatible with *Troilus and Criseyde*, not a determining factor in the construction of the text because it is an idea of storytelling that held little currency in Chaucer's day.

However, finding concepts of narrative more relevant to Chaucer and his works is not simply a matter of approaching a body of contemporary and near-contemporary texts that develop and encourage

---

[1] For opposing sides of the debate, see Victoria Warren, "(Mis)Reading the 'Text' of Criseyde: Context and Identity in Chaucer's *Troilus and Criseyde*", *Chaucer Review* 36 (2001): 1–15 and Jeff Massey, "'The *Double Bind* of Troilus to Tellen': The Time of the Gift in Chaucer's *Troilus and Criseyde*", *Chaucer Review* 38 (2003): 16–35, at 22–3.

[2] Jill Mann, "Troilus' Swoon", *Chaucer Review* 14 (1980): 319–35, Priscilla Martin, *Chaucer's Women: Nuns, Wives and Amazons*. Iowa City, Iowa: University of Iowa Press, 1990: 180–2, and Barry Windeatt, *Troilus and Criseyde*. Oxford: Oxford University Press, 1992: 277–9.

[3] Gregory M. Sadlek, "Love, Labor, and Sloth in Chaucer's *Troilus and Criseyde*", *Chaucer Review* 26 (1992): 350–67.

one particular stylistic paradigm rather than another. Chaucer was not much influenced by the English literary tradition, and when he alludes to a particularly English genre (the tail-rhyme romance), he does so to mock and disparage it. While at the end of *Troilus and Criseyde* he refers favourably to contemporary English writers, who are invited to amend the poem, neither Gower nor Strode provide a theory of vernacular poetry. In any case, Gower's influence on Chaucer is uncertain. Although Chaucer calls him "moral", his own possible adaptation of the *Confessio Amantis* to produce the *Man of Law's Tale* might suggest that his attitude to his contemporary was less absolute, especially if one reads the *Man of Law's Tale* as a criticism of Gower's treatment of Constance.[4] Since the general open-endedness of Chaucer's narratives complicates a simple antithetical reading, the *Man of Law's Tale* is not a particularly useful place to find an absolutist Chaucerian manifesto for (or against) Gower's rhetorical and poetic strategies.

Alternatively, we can have recourse to the rhetorical tradition. In Chapter 1, I suggested that a rhetorical approach to Chaucer's texts provides an understanding of how various ethical and ideological attitudes towards author, audience, and text helps to explain how Chaucer constructs a narrator persona that reflects him as a human being before an audience. In what follows I will attempt to show how Chaucer's alterations and additions to his Italian source text invite a range of perspectives on the story and its characters. These changes urge the audience to identify their personal individual responses and then to compare them with those of others, so as to reach a hermeneutic resolution on the issue of worldly love, while the poem's conclusion encloses this mundane discourse safely within the confines of religious orthodoxy.

Instead of providing entertaining mimesis, *Troilus and Criseyde* becomes a contribution to a cultural discourse that is conscious of its power to create a shared culture by inviting an exchange of perspectives. Chaucer never becomes dogmatic because he encourages individual perspectives based on personal experience over the bookish

---

4   However, this is by no means the only possible reading, as I discuss in the next chapter.

knowledge his poem represents. The poem envisions a society that it serves and creates. Implicitly, Chaucer's position within this community is that of a scholar, author, and servant, who is connected to his audience of courtly lovers by his vicarious experience of love and his ability to give the community of lovers a textual voice.

Narrator and Author

Boccaccio's influence on *Troilus and Criseyde* cannot go ignored. Chaucer's choice of *Il Filostrato* for his source text partly determined the shape of the text, both on the levels of narrative and ideology. Yet the two authors' conclusions could not be more different; while Boccaccio ends by blaming the inconstancy of women for Troilus' downfall, Chaucer blames fortune. Boccaccio's conclusion is made explicit in an apostrophe to young men:

> O giovinetti, ne' quai con l'etate
> surgendo vien l'amoroso disio,
> per Dio vi priego che voi raffreniate
> i pronti passi all'appetito rio,
> e nell'amor di Troiol [sic] vi specchiate,
> il qual dimostra suso il verso mio,
> per che, se ben col cuor gli leggerete,
> non di leggieri a tutte crederete.
> Giovane donna, è mobile e vogliosa
> è negli amanti molti, e sua bellezza
> estima piú ch'allo specchio, e pomposa
> ha vanagloria di sua giovinezza;
> la qual quanto piacevole e vezzosa
> è piú, cotanto piú seco l'apprezza;
> virtú non sente né conoscimento,
> volubil sempre come foglia al vento.

> O youths, in whom amorous desire gradually riseth with age, I pray you for the love of the gods that ye check the ready steps to that evil passion and that ye mirror yourselves in the love of Troilus, which my verses set forth above, for if ye will read them aright and will take them to heart, not lightly will ye have

trust in all women. A young woman is fickle and is desirous of many lovers, and her beauty she esteemeth more than it is in her mirror, and abounding vainglory hath she in her youth, which is all the more pleasing and attractive the more she judgeth it in her own mind. She hath no feeling for virtue or reason, inconstant ever as leaf in the wind. (VIII.225–40)[5]

Chaucer's version has no explicit moral, and the narrative ends on the enigma of Troilus' death and his ascension to Heaven:

> The wrath, as I bigan yow for to seye,
> Of Troilus the Grekis boughten deere,
> For thousandes his hondes maden deye,
> As he that was withouten any peere,
> Save Ector, in his tyme, as I kan heere.
> But – weilawey, save only Goddes wille,
> Despitously hym slough the fierse Achille.
> And whan that he was slayn in this manere,
> His lighte goost ful blisfully is went
> Up to the holughnesse of the eighthe sphere. (V.1800–9)

While Chaucer allows Troilus "no release into the wish-world of metamorphosis",[6] one can argue that he gives him something much greater: a perspective from which the follies of man and the pangs of Fortune cannot reach him. Shortly before his death, the narrator laments that

> Gret was the sorwe and pleynte of Troilus,
> But forth hire cours Fortune ay gan to holde. (V.1744–5)

The curse of Fortune's constant inconstancy, as it were, becomes an irrelevance for Troilus after he has reached "the holughnesse of the eighthe sphere" of the heavens,[7] he is beyond her reach:

[5] I am quoting from B. A. Windeatt, *Geoffrey Chaucer: Troilus and Criseyde, A New Edition of* The Book of Troilus. London: Longman, 1984. The translation is from *Il Filostrato*. Nathaniel Edward Griffin and Arthur Beckwith Myrick (ed. and trans.). Philadelphia, Penn.: University of Pennsylvania Press, 1929.

[6] Winthrop Wetherbee, *Chaucer and the Poets: An Essay on Troilus and Criseyde*. Ithaca, NY, Cornell University Press, 1984: 80.

[7] Karen Elaine Smyth reads this as a movement from the eighth to the ninth sphere, which underpins Chaucer's exploration of "conflicts and irresolution between change and stasis" ("Reassessing Chaucer's Cosmological Discourse

> And down from thennes faste he gan avyse
> This litel spot of erthe that with the se
> Embraced is, and fully gan despise
> This wrecched world, and held al vanite
> To respect of the pleyn felicite
> That is in hevene above; and at the laste,
> Ther he was slayn his lokyng down he caste,
> And in hymself he lough right at the wo
> Of hem that wepten for his deth so faste,
> And dampned al oure werk that foloweth so
> The blynde lust, the which that may nat laste,
> And sholden al oure herte on heven caste (V.1814–25)

Boccaccio ends by blaming women. Chaucer, however, seeks a more abstract, spiritual explanation that demands consideration of how the pitfalls of earthly love relate to divine love. In life, Troilus plays the part of the conventional lover from the moment he sees Criseyde; in death, he is free from arbitrary fortune and mundane vanity.

This paradigmatic shift lead C. S. Lewis to argue for Chaucer's "medievalization" of his Italian original by virtue of added doctrinal concerns and his devotion to the "code of courtly love".[8] Later responses to the text have substantially refined (or refuted) this position with more complex understandings of Chaucer's treatment of the story. But it is undeniable that Boccaccio's more secular ending – his envoy to his lady, with a prayer to Apollo – finds its opposite in Chaucer's rendition, where an almost literal translation of a prayer from Dante's *Paradiso* resolves the text:

> Thow oon, and two, and thre, eterne on lyve,
> That regnest ay in thre, and two, and oon,
> Uncircumscript, and al maist circumscrive,
> Us from visible and invisible foon
> Defende, and to thy mercy, euerichon,
> So make us, Jesus, for thi mercy digne,
> For love of mayde and moder thyn benigne. (V.1863–9)

---

at the End of *Troilus and Criseyde* (c.1385)", *Fifteenth-Century Studies* 32 (2007): 150–63, at 160).

[8] "What Chaucer Really Did to *Il Filostrato*", *Essays and Studies* 17 (1931): 56–75, at 56.

This transcendent resolution explains the human comedy by reminding its audience that, in the end, the love of God is most important, and that the events of this world are laughable from a celestial perspective. It is certainly true that in *Troilus and Criseyde* Chaucer accepts, in the words of A. C. Spearing, "fragmentation, pluralism, and relativism, the 'Diverse folk diversely they seyde' of the *Tales*",[9] but the tolerance of varied opinion remains within the frame of Christian transcendence, even if some find the closure "barely sustained in *Troilus*".[10] Such dismissal of the poem's Christian resolution, hardly Spearing's own,[11] seems unlikely for a fourteenth century English writer; firmer contextual evidence can be found for Peter Dronke's argument that "Chaucer asks the young lovers, both men and women, of his audience, to make the transition that Troilus made" – namely, to abandon "worldly vanyte".[12] This is a wholly orthodox Boethian position.[13]

But to call this *contemptus mundi* would be reductive; the poem allows worldly vanities their limited significance. Karen Smyth notes that Chaucer's description of the porous eighth sphere, the emphasis on mobility, and the absence of the word "firmament" in the passage on Troilus's ascension all imply an affirmation of human and divine love in a "hierarchical ordering that promotes ambiguity through synthesis of the Christian and secular (or pagan) lesson of the narrative".[14] The pluralism of our own world should not blind us to Chaucer's alterity; the fragmentary discourse of individual perspectives at the beginning of the poem can only conclude with the voice of doctrinal authority, as it does in Troilus' ascent and the final prayer to

9   "A Ricardian 'I': The Narrator of *Troilus and Criseyde*", in *Essays in Ricardian Literature*, A. J. Minnis, Charlotte C. Morse, and Thorlac Turville-Petre (eds.). Oxford: Clarendon Press, 1997: 1–22, at 22.
10 Ibid.
11 This critical tradition largely begins with E. T. Donaldson's "The Ending of Chaucer's *Troilus*", in *Early English and Norse Studies Presented to Hugh Smith*, Arthur Brown and Peter Foote (eds.). London: Methuen, 1963: 26–45, esp. 41–5.
12 "The Conclusion of *Troilus and Criseyde*", *Medium Ævum* 1964 (33): 47–52, at 49.
13 Troilus' ascent to the heavenly spheres has its ultimate source in the *Consolation of Philosophy* Book 4, verse 1.
14 "Reassessing Chaucer's Cosmological Discourse", 160.

God, who is "Uncircumscript, and al maist circumscrive". This is a reminder that diverse human voices, however relevant and important in the present world, become irrelevant in the next; even if such an ending hinders the poem's appeal for modern secular critics, its power for a faithful medieval Christian cannot go ignored. There is much irony in *Troilus and Criseyde*, but none, I think, is here.

This Boethian ethos is perhaps Chaucer's greatest addition to *Troilus and Criseyde* and his main criticism of his source text. However, Chaucer does not present his text as a response to Boccaccio; instead, he carefully and frequently tells his English audience that his primary source is a Latin authority – one "Lollius" – and that he is also familiar and comfortable with other histories of Troy. At the beginning of the first *Canticus Troili*, Chaucer devotes a stanza to explaining how his text relates to his Latin *auctor*:

> And of his song naught only the sentence,
> As writ myn auctour called Lollius,
> But pleinly, save oure tonges difference,
> I dar wel seyn, in al, that Troilus
> Seyde in his song, loo, every word right thus
> As I shal seyn; and whoso list it here,
> Loo, next this vers he may it fynden here. (I.393–9)

I agree with A. C. Spearing's suggestion that Chaucer's audience could not have possibly known that this source was invented,[15] and I would argue that the effect of this proclamation for someone who thinks that Lollius was a real, authoritative historian is that Chaucer is providing to his vernacular audience a connection to a reliable narrative of Troilus' love and double sorrow. A. J. Minnis notes that

> Chaucer did not much care what "Omer, Dares and Dite" had actually said; he did not bother to verify the existence of his "auctour Lollius": he wished to use the names of the *auctores*, to "cash in" on their antiquity and *auctoritas*.[16]

As a result, the text appears to be a history.

---

15 *Textualized Subjectivity*, Oxford: Oxford University Press, 2005: 21.
16 *Medieval Theory of Authorship*, 2nd edn. London: Scolar Press, 1988: 210.

In this context, Chaucer's devotion to Lollius confirms his text's veracity. In his claim to translate not just the meaning of his original, but the words themselves, Chaucer promises a reliable and authoritative account which a translation of a near-contemporary Italian source could not provide. On this stanza, David Lawton notes:

> The source for the *Canticus* is not Chaucer's usual source, Boccaccio's *Il Filostrato*, but Petrarch's Sonnet 88, and the translation is close enough to justify Chaucer's claim that he translates "naught only the sentence" but "every word". However, both Petrarch and Boccaccio remain unnamed, here as in the rest of *Troilus*, and the effect of this stanza is therefore to construct a fictional gloss on the English poet's general treatment of his proclaimed Latin source. The implication, I think, is that normally he performs an act of abridgement, rendering Lollius' "sentence"; stencil translation, as here, is the exception.[17]

This representation of the text as an authoritative account puts Chaucer in the position of a scholar whose Latin gives him greater access to texts than that open to his audience.

While Lawton believes that the *Canticus* is an exception, I would argue that this passage is merely one of many rhetorical proclamations that give Chaucer's translation an overt connection to an authoritative textual tradition. Thus in Book II Chaucer writes:

> Wherfore I nyl have neither thank ne blame
> Of al this werk, but prey yow mekely,
> Disblameth me if any word be lame,
> For as myn auctour seyde, so sey I.
> Ek though I speeke of love unfelyngly,
> No wondre is, for it nothyng of newe is;
> A blynd man[18] kan nat juggen wel in hewis. (II.15–21)

Although this is not a claim for "stencil translation", it emphasises Chaucer's marginal agency in the creation of the text and his reliance on books for this story of love. This reliance permeates the poem from

---

17 David Lawton, *Chaucer's Narrators*. Cambridge: D. S. Brewer, 1985: 77.
18 Blindness is often associated with love in the poem – see P. M. Kean, "Chaucer's Dealings with a Stanza of *Il Filostrato* and the Epilogue of *Troilus and Criseyde*", *Medium Ævum* 33 (1964): 36–46, at 40–1.

beginning to end. When his source fails to mention whether Criseyde had children (I.133), how old she was (V.826), or her response to the news that Troilus is out of town (III.575–6), Chaucer cannot fill in the blanks. Of course some of these details are "the inevitable gaps that any historian must put up with",[19] but Chaucer's professed refusal to invent the details of the story implies, much like its cited classical sources, the veracity and authority of its contents.

Books also become a shield used by Chaucer to protect himself from the criticisms of his female audience members:

> Bysechyng every lady bright of hewe,
> And every gentil womman, what she be,
> That al be that Criseyde was untrewe,
> That for that gilt she be nat wroth with me.
> Ye may hire gilt in other bokes se;
> And gladlier I wol write, yif yow leste,
> Penopeës trouthe and good Alceste. (V.1772–8)

Of course, as A. J. Minnis notes, "anyone who has read the actual sources of Chaucer's 'ancient' tale of the love of Troilus knows full well that he can be very cavalier in his treatment of them".[20] But Chaucer's emphasis on his diligent rendition of his original suggests his agency is limited, thus placing him in the familiar position of the medieval compiler or translator.[21] It is certainly true that the compiler's defence was for Chaucer

> an *apologia* for a portrait of pagan society which, in fourteenth-century England, would have been regarded as an historically plausible one, and a method of expressing his detachment from the beliefs of a noble but limited people.[22]

---

19 *Chaucer's Narrators*, 78.
20 *Chaucer and Pagan Antiquity*. Cambridge: D. S. Brewer, 1982: 68.
21 A. J. Minnis suggests that Chaucer's comments on his literary activity at the end of Book II and the end of the poem "have more in common with the prologues of compiling historians like Vincent of Beauvais and Ralph Higden than they have with Gower's prologues" – *Medieval Theory of Authorship*, 210.
22 *Chaucer and Pagan Antiquity*, 67.

At the same time, Chaucer's professed lack of agency and devotion to his source text implies a reliability that will ensure its significance for generations to come.

Further rhetorical moves imply Chaucer's authority without overt ironic gameplay, as in his reference to Dares:

> And if I hadde ytaken for to write
> The armes of this ilke worthi man,
> Than wolde ich of his batailles endite;
> But for that I to writen first bigan
> Of his love, I have seyd as I kan –
> His worthi dedes, whoso list hem heere,
> Rede Dares, he kan telle hem alle ifeere. (V.1765–71)

In a medieval context, this juxtaposition would give an impression of historical veracity and accuracy. In Isidore of Seville's *Etymologiae*, Dares is the second historian of human history (Moses is the first and Herodotus third).[23] Here Chaucer confirms his domain of historical knowledge and expertise alongside his conventional view of Dares as an accepted authority on the Trojan war; the implication is one of association. Chaucer leaves his audience with the impression that they have just been exposed to, as it were, a history of Troilus' love on par with the martial account of humanity's second historian.[24]

Chaucer's role as a transmitter of historical detail is only one side of his claims to textual and historical information. Near the end of the text, he also establishes and confirms his poetic position in English society as an author:

> Go, litel bok, go, litel myn tragedye,
> Ther God thi makere yet, er that he dye,

---

23   Ruth Morse, *Truth and Convention in the Middle Ages: Rhetoric, Representation, and Reality*. Cambridge: Cambridge University Press, 1991: 97.

24   Charles Dahlberg suggests, based upon a close reading of this passage, that "The four-times repeated personal pronoun *I*, particularly in the clause 'I have seyd as I kan', effects a separation of narrator from the narrative of Troilus's struggle and death and underlines the claimed separation between love and war" ("The Narrator's Frame for *Troilus*", *Chaucer Review* 15 (1990): 85–100, at 92–3).

> So sende myght to make in som comedye!
> But litel book, no makyng thow n'envie,
> But subgit be to alle poesye;
> And kis the steppes where as thow seest pace
> Virgile, Ovide, Omer, Lucan, and Stace.
> And for ther is so gret diversite
> In Englissh and in writyng of oure tonge,
> So prey I God that non myswrite the,
> Ne the mysmetre for defaute of tonge;
> And red wherso thow be, or elles songe,
> That thow be understonde, God I biseche! (V.1786–92)

This is Chaucer at his most confident. He envisions his work as part of a tradition that includes the great Latin and Greek authors, whose authority was well established by the late fourteenth century. Boccaccio rarely employs the sort of self-deprecation so often seen in Chaucer's work, yet the Italian text is much more humble, ending with a dedication to the author's lady, in which he prays to Apollo that she receive and enjoy the text:

> Ma guarda che cosi alta imbasciata
> Non facci senza amor, che tu saresti
> Per avventura assai male accettata,
> Ed anche ben senza lui non sapresti.
> Se seco vai, sarai credo onorata:
> Or va': ch'io prego Apollo che ti presti
> Tanto di grazia ch' ascoltata sii,
> E con lieta risposta a me t' invii.
>
> But see to it that thou dost not make so high an embassy without Love, for thou wouldst be perchance quite ill received, and also thou wouldst not have understanding without him. If thou goest with Love, thou wilt, I believe, be honored. Now go, for I pray Apollo to lend thee so much grace that thou mayest be listened to and she may send thee back to me with a happy response. (IX.57–64)

From a modern perspective, such a passage appears to be in the voice of a fictional narrator figure whose affinity to Boccaccio is as close as Trolio, Criseida, or Pandaro. However, this is not the response urged by Boccaccio in the *Proemio*, where he presents his poem as having been written for his lover, Maria d'Aquino as Fiammetta, and the narrator's reference to his lady's departure from Naples to Sannio in the *Proemio* is not necessarily presented as a fiction.[25] While for modern literary critics this might seem to be a crude, autobiographical reading, it is the response which Boccaccio urges upon his reader, and which was widely accepted until relatively recently.[26] While we cannot confirm nor deny the veracity of the situation Boccaccio describes, it is testament to his rhetoric that it was accepted for so long.

Chaucer's explicit interests appear to transcend such personal pursuits, and, unlike Boccaccio, he presents his poem to a larger community, thus embedding into the poem its public reception amongst a group of lovers who experience poetry together. Chaucer's dedication of the poem to Gower and Strode at its end confirms a textual community of a decidedly English nature, in which Chaucer's and his poetry's position is significant. Thorlac Turville-Petre notes that the "first writer in English explicitly to claim status as a national poet is Chaucer at the end of *Troilus and Criseyde*", and his self-representation in the envoy is that of an "audacious" author.[27] In naming a classical tradition, Chaucer implies that his text is a newcomer to a literary corpus whose authority is a given. The phrase "kis the steppes" is, despite its apparent humility, a bold rhetorical move, because it uses the humble style of the Biblical and medieval tradition to create a cultural and textual affinity. Ernst Curtius notes that the humble style was "codified and quantified in numerous rhetorical loci; the most important of these for early Christianity was the devotional formula" not as an expression of humility but as a means of establishing authority.[28] Thus

---

25 Although it probably is – see the Introduction by Robert P. apRoberts and Anna Bruni Seldis in *Il Filostrato*, Vincezo Pernicone (ed.). New York: Garland, 1986: XX–XXV.
26 Ibid.
27 *England the Nation*. Oxford: Oxford University Press, 1996: 216. David Wallace also notes that this is the first time we find a writer considering "the English art of an English writer as poetry" ("Chaucer's Continental Inheritance: The Early Poems and *Troilus and Criseyde*", in *The Cambridge Chaucer Companion*, Piero Boitani and Jill Mann (eds.). Cambridge: Cambridge University Press, 1986: 19–37, at 29).
28 *European Literature and the Latin Middle Ages*. William R. Trask (trans.). New York: Harper & Row, 1953: 407.

Paul's use of phrases like "servus Dei apostolus autem Iesu Christi" (Titus 1:1) can be seen as motivated by a desire to affirm the significance of the epistle that follows. To quote Curtius further:

> expressions like *Dei gratia* or *servus servorum Dei* ... are formulas in which a superior (e.g., a king or pope) proclaims his God-given authority to those beneath him. But the case is quite different when a subject calls himself the thrall, slave, or servant of the king. Here the formula is not one of authority but one of submission.[29]

Much like a king or pope referring to a higher power, Chaucer submits to the authority of classical authors in front of an audience who have limited or no access to them. The effect is to place Chaucer as a mediator between the ancients and those who read or hear the English text, much as a king's *intitulatio* implies his position as a mediator between his subjects and God.

Chaucer's self-identification as the servant of the servants of Love, with its echoes of papal proclamations of power, could not be more apt, since it neatly places Chaucer as the mediator of ideas for those who experience them in their raw, quotidian manifestations. Such a position never becomes one of overt social superiority, since Chaucer emphasises that he cannot dare to love for his "unliklynesse":

> For I, that God of Loves servantz serve,
> Ne dar to Love, for myn unliklynesse,
> Preyen for speed, al sholde I therfore sterve,
> So fer am I from his help in derknesse.
> But natheles, if this may don gladnesse
> Unto any lovere, and his cause availle,
> Have he my thonk, and myn be this travaille! (I.15–21)

This self-marginalisation from the real world is a familiar pose, found in the *Book of the Duchess* to similar effect, in the *Parliament of Fowls*, and, most emphatically, in the *House of Fame*, where the narrator's name (Geffrey) forces even modern critics dedicated to the notion of the narrator as an autonomous fiction to conflate him with Chaucer. Because this voice presents itself as the author of the text, a heavy

---

29   Ibid.

amount of skepticism, counter-intuitive reading, and confidence in the consistent fiction of the text is necessary to distinguish Chaucer from the narrator. However, continuous references to the narrator as the author of the poem encourage our perception of the speaking voice of *Troilus and Criseyde* as the same person who wrote the text, even though we are dealing with Chaucer's social mask. As in the *Legend of Good Women*, the narrator of *Troilus and Criseyde* shows his dedication to love through books, but his position has become that of a writer ("myn be this travaille" – i.e., the poem), instead of a reader who enjoys books more than chess or backgammon, or who reads too much to notice his neighbours. This becomes a position of great authority for Chaucer, and becomes the backdrop for his audacious claim that he is to his culture what Virgil, Ovid, and Homer were to theirs.

Audience

Chaucer invites his audience to compare his reliable account of Troilus' with their experiences as lovers; such interactive reading will result in a communal interpretation of the text's meaning. We get a hint of this debate at the beginning of the poem, where he addresses his audience with an emphasis on their diversity. They are firstly described as "loveres, that bathen in gladnesse" (I.22), then as "hem that ben in the cas/Of Troilus, as ye may after here", and then as "hem that ben despeired/In love, that nevere nyl recovered be" (I.36–7). Chaucer then addresses "hem that ben at ese," (I.43) and "hem that Loves servauntz be" (I.48). These flattering terms identify the audience as courtly lovers in a rhetorical move also found in Chaucer's earlier work, particularly in *Anelida and Arcite*, *Book of the Duchess*, and *Parliament of Fowls*. The audience is diverse, their perspectives are fragmentary, and their access to truth is limited (and, paradoxically, enhanced) by their individuality.

Further on, Chaucer addresses his audience as "Ye wise, proude, and worthi folkes alle" (I.233). While Strohm sees a shift of "a new narrative voice" and, accordingly, a new "imagined audience" in this passage,[30] I see it as another address to the same heterogeneous group of lovers at various points on Fortune's wheel. The audience as a whole are the "wise, proude, and worthi folkes", who are encouraged to

> scornen Love, which that so soone kan
> The fredom of youre hertes to hym thralle;
> For evere it was, and evere it shal byfalle,
> That Love is he that alle thing may bynde,
> For may no man fordon the lawe of kynde. (I.234–8)

As before, the audience is addressed as lovers, but instead of describing their actual situations, here Chaucer applies a judgment that is both moral and pragmatic, if a bit cold. Seen in this light, the passage becomes a shift of approach and attitude that provides various audience members with what seems to be Chaucer's own interpretation of the text, which they can either reject or agree to in their debate on the poem's *sententia*. It is also the poem's overt resolution, possible only because Troilus escapes the concerns of everyday life, freed from Fortune's whims by death and his ascension to Heaven. These passages mark Chaucer's changing method of addressing his audience, but the audience remains the same: they are still lovers who need to be reminded that they have put their hearts in bondage under the power of Love.

While Chaucer imagines personae for his audience, this does not mean that they are autonomous fictions that have no basis in reality, especially since the text is not presented as a fiction. As a rhetorical gesture, these addresses to an audience of lovers invite hearers and readers to take up the positions of the various lovers who serve the God of Love. Those who perceive themselves as happy lovers can interpret the text from their perspective, and those who have loved and lost can read from theirs. It is not unlikely that Chaucer's original audience, both readers and hearers, consisted of both happy and tragic

---

30   *Social Chaucer.* Cambridge, Mass.: Harvard University Press, 55–6.

lovers who would have been ready to perceive the text from these various positions, as Chaucer urges them to do in these apostrophes.[31]

This is the situation imagined in the famous frontispiece in Corpus Christi Cambridge MS 61, where Chaucer is depicted reading aloud from a text to an audience of noblemen and women. The castle in the background, and the idyllic garden in which the company of lovers sit and listen to Chaucer speak from his pulpit of love tell us that this image is an idealisation and not a representation of a real event.[32] However, it is like the image that Chaucer creates for himself and the text at its beginning, when he dons the uniform of the pope of love and addresses various lovers. V. A. Kolve writes of the frontispiece that it portrays Chaucer

> reciting to a courtly company in the grounds of a castle...here we see him concerned not with the transmission of his work to a predicated posterity, but with its publication to his own contemporaries: the poem as process, as literary event, in a social setting.[33]

The function of this frontispiece is not only to represent the audience, but to invite readers of the book to imagine themselves as part of this courtly company. Laura Kendrick suggests that the objective of this illumination is "to persuade the lone reader to imagine himself as part of the audience of the 'tragedy' of *Troilus*."[34] Much the same, *mutatis mutandis*, could be said of Chaucer's rhetorical technique of addressing a diverse audience of lovers: both are invitations to do more than read passively. Both encourage audiences to see themselves as lovers who are in an active dialogue with Chaucer.

---

31 I am not the first to see Chaucer's various addresses to his audience as calls for participation and response; see Dieter Mehl, *Geoffrey Chaucer: An Introduction to his Narrative Poetry*. Cambridge: Cambridge University Press, 1986: Ch. 6.

32 See Derek Pearsall, "The *Troilus* Frontispiece and Chaucer's Audience", *Yearbook of English Studies* 7 (1977): 68–74, and *Troilus and Criseyde, A Facsimile of Corpus Christi College Cambridge MS 61*, M. B. Parkes and Elizabeth Salter (eds. and introduction). Cambridge: D. S. Brewer, 1977: 15–23.

33 *Chaucer and the Imagery of Narrative*. Stanford: Stanford University Press, 1984: 12.

34 "The *Troilus* Frontispiece and the Dramatization of Chaucer's *Troilus*", *Chaucer Review* 22 (1987): 81–93, at 92.

The audience's roles as interpreters are the counterpart to Chaucer's professed role as reporter and compiler. Debate over Chaucer's portrayal of Criseyde and his motivations for writing the *Legend of Good Women* (and, for that matter, its relationship to the reception of *Troilus and Criseyde*) can arise only because Chaucer leaves the issue open to interpretation. As Mark Lambert argues, "[i]t is in good part because the reader must keep reinterpreting her that the entire poem shimmers as it does".[35] Chaucer defends his portrayal of Criseyde by referring his audience to the popular opinion of clerks and books ("Ye may hire gilt in other books se" – V.1776),[36] leaving room for the possibility that his defense is not blind acquiescence to other textual treatments of Criseyde, but an invitation to his audience to engage in a discussion of the portrait of Criseyde offered in books, and, accordingly, to begin to question the ubiquitous authority of the written word, including his own. The fact that his textual authorities are, in effect, untrue, affirms his implicit argument that just because something is written down it is not necessarily true.

To come to this conclusion we must see references to the narrator's part in producing the poem as statements coming from Chaucer himself. For a textual culture acclimated to the context of a single author addressing a singular audience – the "dear reader" of the eighteenth century[37] – the address to a diverse audience of many people appears at first glance to be a literary fiction. But in a culture such as Chaucer's where the enjoyment of literature was primarily public and shared, this address is an act of deixis that identifies various individuals

---

35 "*Troilus*, Books I–III", in *Essays on Troilus and Criseyde*, Mary Salu (ed.). Cambridge: D. S. Brewer, 1979: 105–25, at 105.
36 For readings of this passage that focus on Chaucer's attitude to Criseyde, Troilus, and the issue of gender, see Jill Mann, *Geoffrey Chaucer*. New York, NY: Harvester Wheatsheaf, 1991: 16–19; Elaine Tuttle Hansen, *Chaucer and the Fictions of Gender*. Berkeley, Calif.: University of California Press, 1992: 175–8, Angela Jane Weisl, *Conquering the Reign of Femeny: Gender and Genre in Chaucer's Romance*. Cambridge: D. S. Brewer, 1995: 46–9. On the occasion of the *Legend of Good Women*, see Chapter 3 n.23 above.
37 For a discussion of the rhetorical function of these audience addresses, see Werner Brönnimann-Egger, *The Friendly Reader: Modes of Cooperation Between Eighteenth-Century English Poets and Their Audience*. Tübingen: Stauffenburg-Verlag, 1991.

within an audience and, by virtue of that identification, includes them in the community created by the text. Chaucer's address to the lovers in his audience remains impersonal and vague because it invites men and women to choose their positions within the community at will, while keeping the audience's identities continually open to other readers and future hearers of the text in a way that specific addresses, such as Lydgate's dedication of the *Troy Book* to its patron, Henry V, cannot.

It is thus interesting to note that Chaucer, at one point, moves from the plural hearing audience at the beginning of the poem (and at the end – see V.629, 637) to a general, singular reader:

> Thow, redere, maist thiself ful wel devyne
> That swich a wo my wit kan nat diffyne;
> On ydel for to write it sholde I swynke,
> Whan that my wit is wery it to thynke. (V.270–3)

Joyce Coleman responds to Paul Strohm's attempts "to show that Chaucer migrated away from aurality over the course of writing *Troilus and Criseyde*" by suggesting that, since Chaucer again refers to hearers "a mere 359 lines later",[38] this reference to the reader is "possibly format-neutral",[39] and can thus apply to those reading the text privately, those reading the text aloud, and those hearing the text being read to them. It would not be unprecedented for Chaucer to use "read" in this way. Criseyde's own use of the verb (II.100) is a clear example of its format-neutrality, since she uses it to describe both a prelector's and hearers' simultaneous acts of receiving texts. Yet the singular pronoun that accompanies the vocative "redere" in this passage suggests to me that Chaucer is evoking a different communicative situation, since elsewhere in the poem he uses the second-person plural pronoun to refer to hearers.[40]

---

38 *Public Reading and the Reading Public in Late Medieval England and France.* Cambridge: Cambridge University Press, 1996: 60.
39 Ibid., 60.
40 If this is indeed a reference to silent readers, it does not negate the aural context that envelops the text; the reader referred to here might be a reader of the text to hearers as much as it could be a silent, private reader of the text. Coleman calls this the "first audience" argument – ibid.

Chaucer's invitation to Gower and Strode to amend his work in their capacity as literary-professionals appears to be another address to private readers, even if he does not make the mode of their reading explicit. However, it is at this point that Chaucer refers to the poem as a "book", inviting the image of the two men reading the text alone in manuscript form to make their alterations. Yet this task is not reserved solely for these two men or for private readers. Chaucer also encourages his aural audience to fix his work, because his distance to the experience of love renders his interpretation inferior to theirs:

> For myne wordes, heere and every part,
> I speke hem alle under correccioun
> Of yow that felyng han in loves art,
> And putte it al in youre discrecioun
> To encresse or maken dymynucioun
> Of my langage, and that I yow biseche. (III.1331–6)

Chaucer's reference to himself *speaking* encourages us to imagine him reading aloud to an audience who are given hermeneutic authority over the text's meaning and significance, just as the first stanza of the poem assumes a context of aurality:

> The double sorwe of Troilus to tellen,
> That was the kyng Priamus sone of Troye,
> In lovynge, how his aventures fellen
> Fro wo to wele, and after out of joie,
> My purpos is, er that I parte fro ye. (I.1–5)

Chaucer's uses of the second-person plural pronoun in these passages, and of the plural pronouns when addressing "ye loveres", suggest a communal response and a public reception of the text, and is the standard deictic practice in this poem. This "you" consists of the lovers, both men and women, who can identify with Troilus' experience of love at one stage or another, and whose experience gives them authority to create a communally mediated understanding of the text and its meaning. While Gower and Strode amend the text on one level, they amend it on another.

Conclusions

At the beginning of *Troilus and Criseyde*, Chaucer is careful to position himself and his audience within a communicative situation in which he reports and they are invited to respond. If we see his various addresses as rhetorical representations of his intended audience, who are encouraged to compare their experiences of love to Troilus', the significance of these addresses as part of Chaucer's socialising strategy becomes apparent. Much like the audience of lovers in his earlier poetry, the men and women addressed in *Troilus and Criseyde* are a courtly community by virtue of their relationship to the text and their personal, not textual, understanding of its courtly conventions.

The "I" of *Troilus and Criseyde*, on the other hand, is almost everything but a lover. He serves lovers, although he cannot love; he writes of their culture and contributes to their debate; he even offers a moral condemnation of love, which can either be seen as Chaucer's moral sentiment or another facet of the limited perception of the text's speaking voice.

A reading of this narrative voice as an autonomous fictional character, as real as Troilus, Criseyde, Pandarus, Diomede, or any other character in the poem explains away the complexities of its voice as different elements of characterisation. Yet Chaucer's rhetoric suggests the reliability and historicity of his narrative, providing little ground to read the deictic markers of narrator and audience as literary affectations, since the world of the story is never presented as Chaucer's imagined diegesis. Such a modern reading also fails to explain the rhetorical impetus behind Chaucer's proclamation that he is an English poet who will follow in the footsteps of the ancient *auctores*, and also provides a rather prosaic interpretation of a dynamic character whose emotional engagement in the story of the poem has often been noted,[41] particularly since the narrator's emotional response is often related to his act of writing:

---

41   This can perhaps best be summarised by Thomas H. Bestul's observation that we "learn, mainly in the proems to the first four books, of the narrator's ambitions, his inadequacies, and his difficulties, but also of his feelings as he nar-

> From Troilus she [Fortune] gan hire brighte face
> Awey to writhe, and tok of hym non heede,
> But caste hym clene out of his lady grace,
> And on hire whiel she sette up Diomede;
> For which myn herte right now gynneth blede,
> And now my penne, allas, with which I write,
> Quaketh for drede of that I moste endite. (IV.8–14)

E. T. Donaldson's conception of an unreliable narrator, manipulated "to achieve the poetic expression of an extraordinarily complex" view that is Chaucer's (and not the narrator's), demands that we distinguish between the voice of the poet and the voice of the narrator.[42] In passages such as this, such a distinction is impossible – is Chaucer's fourteenth century audience being invited to imagine a fictional, unreliable narrator writing the poem being read aloud by Chaucer? Is this "simple" narrator, as Donaldson would have it,[43] also the same person who claims his place as a national poet descending from Virgil, Ovid, and Homer?

Alternatively, the narrator's emotional engagement and poetic activity can be seen as an expression of Chaucer's own relationship to his text. Elizabeth Salter criticises Donaldson's view by interpreting the narrator's commentary of *Troilus and Criseyde* as a record of

> the poet's busy – and sometimes not entirely happy – engagement with his medieval materials, with his medieval public. It records also the poet's struggle to express something of what he dimly understood about the new kind of life he had given to his characters.[44]

---

rates the story of Troilus. While it is true that Chaucer emphasizes the cultural and historical distance between his narrator and the main story ... at the same time it is also true that from the very first stanza Chaucer presents a narrator emotionally moved by the sadness of the events he relates" ("Chaucer's *Troilus and Criseyde*: The Passionate Epic and its Narrator", *Chaucer Review* 14 (1980): 366–78, at 368).

42 "The Ending of Chaucer's *Troilus*", 43.
43 Ibid.
44 "*Troilus and Criseyde*: Poet and Narrator", in *Acts of Interpretation*, Mary J. Carruthers and Elizabeth D. Kirk (eds.). Norman, Oklahoma: Pilgrim, 1982: 281–91, at 290.

This record of the poet's experiences shifts the audience's attention increasingly upon the process of producing the poem, and, thus, to that agency that Chaucer so frequently denies himself. I would add that these concerns, centred around the axis of poetic communication, are embedded within the narrative at every turn because the narrator is Chaucer's self-representation.

A. C. Spearing has offered an alternative understanding of the text as a poem with no voice. He criticises the assumption that "a written story must have a teller",[45] suggesting instead that the first-person pronoun of the poem varies in reference to give "access to fragments of a merely putative unitary truth".[46] A rhetorical reading of this speaking voice as a representation of Chaucer is complementary to such an interpretation, although fundamentally different. If the poem is seen as a text written for oral performance, both by Chaucer and by others who would see the poem as a textual reproduction of Chaucer's voice, its first-person pronoun has the clear deictic function of representing the speaking voice of the author; as Spearing himself notes, in "spoken narrative, as in speech generally, the first person is anchored materially to the body from which the speaking voice issues, and continuity of reference for first-person pronouns is guaranteed by the reciter's physical presence".[47]

While Spearing does not admit this context for the poem, it would be congruent with Chaucer's references to aurality, Joyce Coleman's research of the period, the specific context I have argued for *Book of the Duchess*, and the Augustinian and Boethian conception of letters as representations of the absent voice discussed in Chapter 3. If *Troilus and Criseyde* was written first for an act of auto-prelection and secondly for public and private reading, its many narrative voices can be understood as various rhetorical gestures within a narrator-persona that is not the victim of Chaucer's irony, or an ontologically whole fiction, but a rhetorical representation of Chaucer himself. The persona is not consistent, because rhetorical masks must vary and change to have an impact on a diverse audience whose re-

---

45   "A Ricardian 'I'", 18.
46   Ibid., 22.
47   Ibid., 18.

sponses to the text will vary. Thus Cicero describes a four-fold approach of gaining an audience's benevolence by defining different *loci* for the speaker to exploit:

> Benevolentia quattuor ex locis comparatur: ab nostra, ab adversariorum, ab iudicum persona, a causa. Ab nostra, si de nostris factis et officiis sine arrogantia dicemus; ... si, quae incommoda acciderint aut quae instent difficultates, proferemus; si prece et obsecratione humili ac suppplici utemur.

> Good-will is to be had from four quarters: from our own person, from the person of the opponents, from the persons of the jury, and from the case itself. We shall win good-will from our own person if we refer to our own acts and services without arrogance; ... if we dilate on the misfortunes which have befallen us or the difficulties which still beset us; if we use prayers and entrieties with a humble and submissive spirit.[48]

Speakers may adopt a variety of approaches, choosing to affirm authority by their social position and deeds at one moment, and to admit humility and submission to the power of the audience at another. Admittedly, Chaucer's rhetorical self-representation does not seem to revolve around an axis of political power (although he does ostensibly defer to an orthodox social hierarchy in the *Canterbury Tales*, when he famously apologises for not putting "folk in hir degree" with the excuse "My wit is short, ye may wel understonde" at I.744–6). However, some such understanding of an orator's self-representation does explain the seemingly inconsistent variations in the narrative voice as different rhetorical gestures that develop and influence an audience's experience of the text and its author. In *Troilus and Criseyde*, Chaucer's rhetorical self-representation moves hermeneutic authority away from himself while affirming his social significance as a redactor of classical texts and as an author of English poetry for an English community. But while Chaucer begins the discussion, his audience must finish it.

---

48   *De Inventione* XVI.22, translation by H. M. Hubbell in *De Inventione, De Optimo Genere Oratorum and Topica.* Cambridge: Harvard University Press, 1949, 45.

Chapter 5
The Storyteller: The *Thopas-Melibee* Link

Chaucer the Pilgrim?

Somewhere within the frame structure of the *Canterbury Tales* is the narrator, ambiguously situated between the text's real-world audience and the fictional pilgrims on their way to Canterbury. Chaucer's audience can catch a glimpse of the pilgrims only through the narrator's gaze, which the ironic subtext of the *General Prologue* suggests is limited. Jill Mann notes that the narrator describes the pilgrims as professional types in their own language; thus "[a]ll excellence becomes 'tricks of the trade' – and this applies to the Parson's virtues as well as to the Miller's thefts". It is this limited viewpoint, Mann argues, that forces us to consider the pilgrims on their own terms, without a "*systematic* application of moral judgments".[1] Unlike Gower's *Confessio Amantis*, the *Canterbury Tales* does not provide an ethical code with which one may judge the characters in the poem for their moral and social failings; such a code must ultimately come from an individual audience member's personal ideological view.

For Chaucer's audience, this would have been a medieval Christian view, and Chaucer may have encouraged a Christian attitude of forgiveness with his limited narratorial voice. Donald R. Howard suggests that the narrator's obtuseness has an Augustinian, Christian function, namely to present merely the "surface appearance" which allows "the pilgrims themselves [to] show the underlying reality" of their humanity.[2] We get from the narrator only a limited insight into the characters as types, whereas the tales themselves and the inter-

---

[1] Jill Mann. *Chaucer and Medieval Estates Satire.* Cambridge: University Press, 1973: 194, italics in the original.
[2] Donald Howard, "Chaucer the Man", *PMLA* 80 (1965): 337–43, at 343.

ludes within the frame-tale inform us of their idiosyncrasies and individuality. While Chaucer's audience passes judgment upon the pilgrims for their vices, the narrator refrains (or pretends to refrain), perhaps, as Howard suggests, because he is too obtuse to do so: "in the masquerade of the literal-minded, gregarious pilgrim, Chaucer plays a kind of Holy Fool who stumbles into Christian charity unawares".[3] While we perceive the "intellectual errors" of the narrator, as Howard would have it, those same errors force us to see the "created man beneath the canker evil" even in the Monk or the Pardoner.[4] According to Howard, the narrator presents each pilgrim in the language of his or her own class, without judgment or condemnation, and this seemingly objective account forces us to empathise, if but for a moment, with the characters. In this act of empathy, we stop seeing them as types and begin seeing them as human beings, warts and all. Such a reading is reminiscent of the anti-rationalism of Bernard of Clairvaux (see for example *De amore Dei*), whom Chaucer quotes in the *Parson's Tale*,[5] and who could have been one of Chaucer's inspirations for presenting his flawed characters. Accordingly, the narrator's limited viewpoint allows him an innocent sympathy for the failings of humanity.

The theory of the narrator as a "Holy Fool" helps us to understand his attitude towards some pilgrims; with others, it is less helpful. To take the famous example of the Monk, we learn that

> He yaf nat of that text [the Benedictine Rule] a pulled hen,
> That seith that hunters ben nat hooly men,
> Ne that a monk, whan he is recchelees,
> Is likned til a fissh that is waterlees –
> This is to seyn, a monk out of his cloystre.
> But thilke text heeld he nat worth an oystre;
> And I seyde his opinion was good. (I.177–83)

Chaucer's choice to criticise the Monk's hypocrisy by ironically acquiescing to it is an acknowledgement of his function as a mediator between his characters and an external value-system. Medieval estates

---

3   Ibid.
4   Ibid.
5   See, for example, X.130, 166, 253–5, and 256.

satire typically mocks monks' "love of good food, luxurious clothing, a love of horses and hunting, contempt for patristic and monastic authority, laziness, a refusal to stay within cloister walls, the temptations of holding various monastic offices".[6] Such a tradition was as fresh in Chaucer's intended audience's mind as it is distant from our own modern world. Engrossed in such a tradition, Chaucer's audience would recognise his criticism of the Monk for what it is: biting social satire which is neither entirely new nor socially disruptive.[7] This is not to say that Chaucer was incapable of seeing through the sin and feeling a sympathetic, Christian love for the man underneath; the *Parson's Tale* in particular suggests that he had high hopes for the spiritual well-being of his audience. Yet that suggestion of penitence and forgiveness comes at the end of the work and not at the beginning, where the follies of everyday life are expressed by the conventions of estates satire.

The humanitarian, Christian effort Chaucer makes in getting his audience to appreciate the humanity of some of his characters is nonetheless a central feature of much of the *General Prologue*. Chaucer's descriptions of his pilgrims often present the world "as it is," hence Mann's and Howard's observations that the narrator stops short of judging the characters by absolute values; such an approach would limit the audience's interpretative power over the text by disallowing individual responses. The audience is invited to laugh at a monk who will not follow the mendicant order

> Or swynken with his handes, and laboure,
> As Austyn bit? How shal the world be served?
> Lat Austyn have his swynk to hym reserved! (I.186–8)

---

6 *Chaucer and Medieval Estates Satire*, 17.
7 Gerald Morgan suggests that we should not see Chaucer as a "reactionary", because such a judgment would assert "a political agenda of which he may be entirely innocent, but we do have to recognize and come to terms with the settled aristocratic assumptions and perspectives out of which he writes" ("Moral and Social Identity and the Idea of Pilgrimage in the *General Prologue*", *Chaucer Review* 37 (2003): 285–314, at 286).

At the same time, they are invited to judge him as they see fit. I would suggest that Chaucer allows this clearly ironic judgment because the Monk's hypocrisy is so obvious, and his character so conventional, that there is little chance that the author's implied response will contradict that of his audience, particularly if they are familiar with such hawking, indolent monks, either from texts or real-life. The heavily laden irony of the narrator's description of the Monk refers to a clash between the Monk's behaviour and his station, which for Chaucer and his audience was obvious, and the narrator's assent is clearly not expressed to evoke sympathy for the poor Monk, but to remind the audience of Chaucer's ethical position inside and outside the text. The poet's dual-presence allows him a space both to judge his characters and influence his audience by embedding that judgment into the text's rhetorical fabric.

For too long Chaucerians have indulged in the false dilemma of whether the first-person pronoun of the *General Prologue* refers to the author or the naive narrator. In many discussions of the *General Prologue*, the narrator is considered a composite entity, both a fiction removed from Chaucer himself and an omniscient narrator who is familiar with intimate details about the pilgrims, such as the Prioress's French lessons and the Miller's dubious business practices. The narrator's seemingly limited perspective on the one hand and his omniscience on the other resist a resolution for the reader expecting stylistic consistency and a coherent narrative unit. But rhetorical masks are by definition ever changing and inconsistent because they are not created to produce the illusion of an autonomous fiction. As representations of the author or speaker, the dynamism of the rhetorical mask allows one's self-representation to transform to whatever form best suits the situation at hand or the desired rhetorical effect.

Much work has been done on the narrative voice of the *Canterbury Tales,* and it would be impossible to revisit all of the many issues addressed by scholars. For my purposes of highlighting Chaucer's narrative persona as a rhetorical game and not a literary or stylistic device, the *Thopas-Melibee* link is most relevant, and I will focus on the relationship between these two tales. However, to unravel Chaucer's depiction of himself as a writer and a voice for his audience, one must begin before the *Canterbury Tales* and observe how the *Prologue* to the *Legend of Good Women* portrays a writer who is both deeply self-conscious and increasingly confident in his socio-literary position and the importance of his texts to the artistic development of his society's literary culture. In the *Prologue* to the *Man of Law's Tale* Chaucer again returns to a consideration of himself as a secular author for a secular society with even greater confidence. I hope to demonstrate that, in light of these texts, the *Thopas-Melibee* link presents Chaucer as a writer who can inspire a sophisticated public discourse on individual and social ethics and the virtues of political temperance and prudence.

Authorial Representation Inside and Outside the Narrative Voice: Chaucer's Catalogues

We have seen how, in his earlier poetry, Chaucer rhetorically distances himself from society by evoking his asocial reading habits. In his later poetry, we find him identifying himself more as a writer than a reader; in the *Prologue* to the *Legend of Good Women* and the *Prologue* to the *Man of Law's Tale* he suggests a relationship between his literary career and the text at hand that depends upon his pre-existing status as a laureate poet.

In the *Legend of Good Women*, the God of Love accuses the narrator of offending him by translating the *Roman de la rose* which, he says, "is an heresye ayeins my lawe" (F.330 and G.256). The narrator is also to blame for defaming Criseyde:

> And of Creseyde thou hast seyd as the lyste,
> That maketh men to wommen lasse triste,
> That ben as trewe as ever was any steel. (F.332–5)

Not only is this passage a distinct marker that the narrator should be conflated with Chaucer (cf. the "Geffrey" in the *House of Fame*), but it also describes him as a gossip who has made inflammatory state-

135

ments against Criseyde's character. In the later G-version, the narrator's offence takes on a more literary character:

> Hast thow nat mad in Englysh ek the bok
> How that Crisseyde Troylus forsok,
> In shewynge how that wemen han don mis?
> But natheles, answere me now to this;
> Why noldest thow as wel [han] seyd goodnesse
> Of wemen, as thow hast seyd wikednesse?
> Was there no good matere in thy mynde,
> Ne in alle thy bokes ne coudest thow nat fynde
> Som story of wemen that were goode and trewe?
> Yis, God wot, sixty bokes olde and newe
> Hast thow thyself, alle ful of storyes grete. (G.264–74)

No longer a gossip who has *seyd* amiss, Chaucer's crime has become more severe because he has defamed her in his book, which will remain longer within English culture than ephemeral speech. Of course the difference between the versions is not absolute – in both the narrator is identified as a writer – but an emphasis on the offence as a literary act is absent from the F-text, while the G-text characterises further the narrator as a literary-professional.

In both versions Alceste is quick to defend the narrator by cataloguing those of Chaucer's literary texts that cannot offend the God of Love:

> He made the bok that highte the Hous of Fame,
> And ek the Deth of Blaunche the Duchesse,
> And the Parlement of Foules, as I gesse,
> And al the love of Palamon and Arcite
> Of Thebes, thogh the storye is knowen lite;
> And many an ympne for your halydays,
> That highten balades, roundels, vyrelayes;
> And, for to speke of other besynesse,
> He hath in prose translated Boece,
> And Of the Wreched Engendrynge of Mankynde,
> As man may in Pope Innocent yfynde;
> And mad the lyf also of Seynt Cecile.
> He made also, gon is a gret while,
> Orygenes upon the Maudeleyne. (G.405–18, cf. F.417–27)

Whereas Geffrey and the narrators of the *Book of the Duchess* and *Parliament of Fowls* are readers, here we find Chaucer confidently identifying himself as an author and translator for his culture, as he also does in the God of Love's speech in the G-version. Alceste makes it clear that her defence of the narrator depends upon the social function of his texts, which help him to make "lewed folk to delyte/ To serven yow [the God of Love], in preysynge of youre name" (G.403–4; cf. F.415–16). Not unlike the Pope of Love of *Troilus and Criseyde*, the narrator of the *Legend of Good Women* has served the God of Love by serving his servants.

Alceste's defence falls short of praising Chaucer's literary style. In the F-version, she says that he writes poorly ("Al be hit that he kan nat wel endite" F.414), which is an echo of the attitudes towards the narrator of the Eagle in *House of Fame* and of Scipio in *Parliament of Fowls*. However, in the G-version, the comment is softened: "But wel I wot, with that he can endyte" (G.402). While his transgression has moved from an oral to a literate modality, his abilities as a poet become less open to contempt. Elsewhere, Alceste's disdain for the narrator as a poet remains consistent in the two texts:

> And eke, peraunter, for this man ys nyce,
> He myghte doon yt, gessyng no malice,
> But for he useth thynges for to make;
> Hym rekketh noght of what matere he take. (F.362–5)

> Or elles, sire, for that this man is nyce,
> He may translate a thyng in no malyce,
> But for he useth bokes for to make,
> And taketh non hed of what matere he take. (G.340–3)

Chaucer did not alter Alceste's protest that the narrator might have offended the God of Love and women out of simple-mindedness. This apology was not necessarily voiced only for the God of Love; Chaucer's intended audience could also see this as his expression of remorse for the offensive elements of his poetry, and audience members who had been offended, possibly including Queen Anne,[8] could choose to see this as an apology and accept it. The *Legend of Good Women* presents itself as penance for slandering women, and there is no reason to doubt that this element of the text would make it more agreeable and relevant to Chaucer's female audience members.[9]

In much the same manner as *House of Fame* and, more implicitly, *Troilus and Criseyde*, the *Prologue* to the *Legend of Good Women* defines Chaucer's relationship to Love as essentially textual. But the Man of Law, in the prologue to his tale, presents Chaucer as a writer of more than love stories for an English audience. After the Host asks him to tell a tale, the Man of Law says:

> "Hooste," quod he, "*depardieux*, ich assente;
> To breke forward is nat myn entente.
> Biheste is dette, and I wole holde fayn
> Al my biheste, I kan no bettre sayn.
> For swich lawe as a man yeveth another wight,
> He sholde hymselven usen it, by right;
> Thus wole oure text. But nathelees, certeyn,
> I kan right now no thrifty tale seyn
> That Chaucer, thogh he kan but lewedly
> On metres and on rymyng craftily,
> Hath seyd hem in swich Englissh as he kan
> Of olde tyme, as knoweth many a man;
> And if he have noght seyd hem, leve brother,
> In o book, he hath seyd hem in another.
> For he hath toold of loveris up and doun
> Mo than Ovide made of mencioun
> In his Epistles, that been ful olde.
> What sholde I tellen hem, syn they been tolde?" (II.39–56)

---

[8] Many early Chaucerians believed the poem was written for Queen Anne on the basis of Lydgate's statement in the Introduction to the *Fall of Princes* that Chaucer wrote it "at the request of the queene". John Fisher provides a summary of this critical tradition in "The Legend of Good Women", in *Companion to Chaucer Studies*, Beryl Rowland (ed.). Oxford: Oxford University Press, 1968: 464–76, at 464–71.

[9] On fifteenth century female readers of the *Legend of Good Women*, see Nicola McDonald, "Chaucer's *Legend of Good Women*, Ladies at Court and the Female Reader", *Chaucer Review* 35 (2000): 22–42.

On its most superficial level, the comment "Chaucer, thogh he kan but lewedly / On metres and on rymyng craftily, / Hath seyd hem in swich Englissh as he kan" is, like Alceste's remarks, a jab at Chaucer's artistic abilities, and as such this utterance can be seen as Chaucer's comical self-deprecation. We should also consider the Man of Law's disparaging remark in light of his character. He is the same wealthy, materialistic lawyer who "[f]or his science and for his heigh renoun,/Of fees and robes hadde he many oon" (I.316–17). And while debate on the Man of Law's character and his tale continues,[10] it is obvious that the reverence and awe Alceste's speeches and character invite are not met by a similar aura around the Man of Law, who is quite literally more human.[11] To see him as such is to see the greatest part of this self-referential joke (which we will see enacted again with Harry Bailly): the puppet is mocking his master, and Chaucer's audience is invited to laugh at the absurdity of a fictional character mocking his creator. It is also possible that this passage is a sign of the Man of Law's bad taste, or that he is an incompetent reader,[12] since he calls the *Book of the Duchess* a story "of Ceys and Alcione", which Chaucer made "in youthe" (II.57), even though that poem is really about the Duke and Duchess of Lancaster, as Alceste notes in the *Prologue* to the *Legend of Good Women*. If his viewpoint is limited, the Man of Law's judgment is suspect and open to disagreement in a way that the Black Knight's, the Eagle's, Africanus', and Alceste's disparagements are not.[13]

---

10   Most recently, A. C. Spearing has argued that the poetic grace and profound theology of the *Man of Law's Tale* deserve reconsideration, and that the fluidity of the tale's narrative perspectives invite multiple emotional responses – see *Textual Subjectivity*. Oxford: Oxford University Press, 2005: Ch. 4.
11   Florence Percival argues that Alceste represents the "transcendental marguerite of French lyric poetry" – see *Chaucer's Legendary Good Women*. Cambridge: Cambridge University Press, 1998: 43.
12   Rodney Delasanta explores this argument and its relevance to the Man of Law's tale – see "And of Great Reverence: Chaucer's Man of Law", *Chaucer Review* 5 (1971): 288–310.
13   However, A. C. Spearing attacks this view of the Man of Law, defending the tale (and thus its teller) on its stylistic and emotive accomplishments – see *Textual Subjectivity*, 110–15 and 130–6.

The Man of Law also compares Chaucer to Ovid, although he does not go so far as to say whether Chaucer is any better or worse than the Latin poet. But the mere presence of the comparison is significant because it implies that Chaucer has already become an established man of letters for the Man of Law and his fellow pilgrims within the fiction of the tale and for Chaucer's intended audience in the real world. Chaucer's name is cultural currency and he has become an authoritative writer for the English – even if not a very good one. The adverbial phrase "Of olde tyme" (i.e., "long ago") is employed to describe his authorial career, bringing to Chaucer the authority of establishment and literary tradition. For the Man of Law, he has been around for so long that he has already told all the stories appropriate for the Canterbury pilgrimage. For Chaucer, his reputation has become such that he can compare himself with confidence to Ovid and invite his audience to make a similar comparison. If he writes poorly, he is still a literary figure for the English in the Man of Law's mind, and in this passage Chaucer not only reaffirms his authorial status, but uses it as the basis for a metafictional joke, the butt of which is the Man of Law, not Chaucer or the narrator.

The Man of Law continues by listing a catalogue of tales of virtuous women from Chaucer's *Legend of Good Women* and Ovid's *Heroides*:

> "In youthe he made of Ceys and Alcione,
> And sitthen hath he spoken of everichone,
> Thise noble wyves and thise loveris eke.
> Whoso that wole his large volume seke,
> Cleped the Seintes Legende of Cupide,
> Ther may he seen the large woundes wyde
> Of Lucresse, and of Babilan Tesbee;
> The swerd of Dido for the false Enee;
> The tree of Phillis for hire Demophon;
> The pleinte of Dianire and of Hermyon,
> Of Adriane, and of Isiphilee –
> The bareyne yle stondynge in the see –
> The dreynte Leandre for his Erro;
> The teeris of Eleyne, and eek the wo
> Of Brixseyde, and of the, Ladomya;
> The crueltee of the, queene Medea,

> Thy litel children hangynge by the hals,
> For thy Jason, that was of love so fals!
> O Ypermystra, Penelopee, Alceste,
> Youre wifhod he comendeth with the beste!" (II.57–76)

No distinction is made between which tales are Chaucer's and which are Ovid's, and the intermixing of the two forces those who do not know Chaucer's works to conflate the output of both writers. On the one hand, this can appear to be Chaucer's reassertion of his own literary reputation – he has become, in the context of an English literary culture, an authority. On the other hand, the muddled list can, as Delasanta argues, reflect the Man of Law's own affected literary taste, which allows him to confuse two authors because he has not really read either.[14]

The catalogue not only connects Chaucer to Ovid as a literary figure; it also reasserts Chaucer's position as a moral writer who defends women. In the Man of Law's opinion, this is to be contrasted with Gower:

> "But certeinly no word ne writeth he
> Of thilke wikke ensample of Canacee,
> That loved hir owene brother synfully –
> Of swiche cursed stories I sey fy! –
> Or ellis of Tyro Appollonius,
> How that the cursed kyng Antiochus
> Birafte his doghter of hir maydenhede,
> That is so horrible a tale for to rede,
> Whan he hir threw upon the pavement.
> And therefore he, of ful avysement,
> Nolde nevere write in none of his sermons
> Of swiche unkynde abhomynacions,
> Ne I wol noon reherce, if that I may." (II.77–89)

The barb in these references is that the Man of Law finds Gower's stories "cursed" and distasteful. Yet Chaucer found at least the tale of Canacee perfectly tellable, since the *Legend of Good Women* (F.265 and G.219) suggests that he planned to include her story in that collection. Elizabeth Allen argues that Chaucer criticises not the tale it-

---

14 "And of Great Reverence", 288–310.

self, but Gower's method of telling it; accordingly, the technique of the *Confessio Amantis* leads unsophisticated readers such as the Man of Law astray.[15] The fact that Chaucer possibly used Gower as a source for the *Man of Law's Tale*[16] might suggest that it is here being presented as a corrective (whether successful or not), and Chaucer's revision of the tale reflects issues of rhetorical representation latent in the two stories told by the *Canterbury Tales*' narrator.

The alternative is also possible: perhaps this is another joke at the Man of Law's expense. Perhaps Gower really is moral, as Chaucer insists in *Troilus and Criseyde*, and the Man of Law misunderstands the ethical dimension of Gower's text. In either case, Chaucer here refers to his literary output and that of one of his contemporaries and of Ovid to engage a discussion of proper storytelling and literary canons. While Chaucer's exact position on the issue is not immediately obvious to us, the presence of such discourse implies Chaucer's self-consciousness and confidence as a literary figure.

The Botched Tale and the *Litel Tretys*: Persona Play in the *Thopas-Melibee* Link

The joke of the *Tale of Sir Thopas* is that it is drivel being recited by Chaucer's stand-in – and Chaucer is obviously a much more capable author. Can we understand this as self-deprecating rhetoric if it assumes Chaucer's own literary prowess? Is the *Thopas-Melibee* link actually self-deprecating? Or is it an expression of snobbish contempt for the tail-rhyme romances, which are beneath the level of sophisti-

---

[15] Elizabeth Allen, "Chaucer Answers Gower: Constance and the Trouble with Reading", *ELH* 64 (1997): 627–55.

[16] Peter Nicholson, "Chaucer Borrows from Gower: The Sources of the *Man of Law's Tale*", in *Chaucer and Gower: Difference, Mutability, Exchange* R. F. Yeager (ed.). Victoria: University of Victoria, 1991: 85–99 and Peter Nicholson, "The Man of Law's Tale: What Chaucer Really Owed to Gower", *Chaucer Review* 26 (1991): 153–74.

cation normally provided by Chaucer and expected by his superior audience?

As a straightforward tale, *Thopas* is "rym dogerel", but as a parody and self-highlighting joke, it is magnificent. Perhaps because the joke depends on the relationship between Chaucer the real-world figure and the narrator-persona, the irony of the tale is literally beyond Harry Bailly's realm, or perhaps his response is meant to frame our appreciation of his flawed character (as an innkeeper, his marginal social status already makes him dubious), thus preparing us for his flawed interpretation of *Melibee*.

Although we cannot always trust the Host's opinions, few would disagree with his contempt for the poem as a romance. Even Alan T. Gaylord's much more favourable evaluation depends upon relating it to the *Tale of Melibee* and to what Gaylord sees as a deliberate distinction on Chaucer's part between the "sentence" of the *Tale of Melibee* and the "solace" of the *Tale of Sir Thopas*.[17] But even Gaylord's juxtaposition of the two insists that both are found wanting, and the fault of *Thopas* is its fruitless and frivolous discourse.

Because *Thopas* is obviously intentionally a bad tale, it is best perceived as a parody of a literary genre already in place. J. A. Burrow observes that the structure of the poem is a numerological joke, since the diminution of the stanza-form is a harmonious ratio "quite uncharacteristic of the minstrel and ballad poetry which *Thopas* appears to represent",[18] making it fit within an earlier tradition of parody.[19] John Finlayson takes the parody of *Thopas* as a basis for defining *romance* as a genre.[20] Nancy Bradbury has taken the link between *Thopas* and romance further, suggesting that it mocks a tradition to which Chaucer

---

17　Alan Gaylord, "Chaucer's Dainty 'Dogerel': The 'Elvyssh' Prosody of *Sir Thopas*", *Studies in the Age of Chaucer* 1 (1979): 83–104.
18　J. A. Burrow, "*Sir Thopas*: An Agony in Three Fits", *Review of English Studies* 22 (1971): 54–8, at 57–8.
19　J. A. Burrow, "Chaucer's *Sir Thopas* and *La Prise de Nuevile*", *Yearbook of English Studies* 14 (1984): 44–55.
20　John Finlayson, "Definitions of Middle English Romance: Part I", *Chaucer Review* 15 (1980): 44–62 and John Finlayson, "Definitions of Middle English Romance: Part II", *Chaucer Review* 15 (1980): 168–81.

himself contributed with *Troilus and Criseyde*.[21] Similarly, V. J. Scattergood argues that the poem is a burlesque, satirical romance,[22] while T. L. Burton sees in the arming scene a repetitive style that parodies similar scenes in other Middle English romances.[23]

We find Thopas described in a comical affectation of the tailrhyme romances throughout the tale.[24] For example:

> Yborn he was in fer contree,
> In Flaundres, al biyonde the see,
> At Poperyng, in the place.
> His fader was a man ful free,
> And lord he was of that contree,
> As it was Goddes grace.
>
> Sir Thopas wax a doghty swayn;
> Whit was his face as payndemayn,
> His lippes rede as rose;
> His rode is lyk scarlet in grayn,
> And I yow telle in good certayn
> He hadde a semely nose. (VII.718–29)

While the quotidian and mercantile Flemish setting distances the poem and its title character from the dignity of the aristocracy, the effeminate imagery of this passage turns the romance convention of masculine chivalry on its head, and Thopas's masculinity diminishes even further throughout the poem.[25] But he is not only emasculated;

21 Nancy Mason Bradbury, "Chaucerian Minstrelsy: *Sir Thopas, Troilus and Criseyde* and English Metrical Romance", in *Tradition and Transformation in Medieval Romance*, Rosalind Field (ed.). Cambridge: D. S. Brewer, 1999: 115–24.
22 V. J. Scattergood, "Chaucer and the French War: *Sir Thopas* and *Melibee*", in *Court and Poet*, Glyn S. Burgess (ed.). Liverpool: Cairns, 1981: 287–96.
23 T. L. Burton, "Chaucer's *Tale of Sir Thopas*", *Explicator* 40 (1982): 4.
24 For the poem's possible connection to *Guy of Warwick*, see Alan Gaylord, "The Moment of Sir Thopas: Towards a New Look at Chaucer's Language", *Chaucer Review* 16 (1982): 311–29. J. A. Burrow also notes echoes of *Bevis of Hampton* in *Thopas* ("Agony in Three Fits", 56).
25 Jeffrey Jerome Cohen, "Diminishing Masculinity in Chaucer's *Tale of Sir Thopas*", in *Masculinities in Chaucer: Approaches to Maleness in the* Canterbury Tales *and* Troilus and Criseyde, Peter G. Beidler (ed.). Cambridge: D. S. Brewer, 1998: 143–55.

he is also described as a puppet[26] and as a child.[27] In this Chaucer's characterisation of Thopas mirrors the Gawain-poet's description of Arthur's court, whom the Green Knight insults by saying it is full of "berdlez chylder" (1.280).[28]

Although dedicated to subverting romantic expectations, the tale also incorporates an interest in the relationship between storytelling and stories themselves that transcends generic parsing and the tale's relationship to the romance tradition. Ruth Waterhouse and Gwen Griffiths believe that the tale is a parody because its discourse is subordinate to the plot – that is, the central focus of the tale is on what Thopas does.[29] Martin Stevens qualifies this view by arguing that *Thopas* reflects Chaucer's concern with, as he calls it, "narratological competence";[30] for Stevens, *Thopas* demonstrates how a lack of care for narrative structure can cause a story to collapse, since Chaucer's usual attention to the structure of a narrative is deliberately lacking in this short romance. A comparison with *Troilus and Criseyde* brings this point to the fore; whereas the five books of *Troilus and Criseyde* divide it into easily definable sections that can function as individual thematic units, the fits of *Thopas* seem to be inserted not to structure the tale, but, as Burrow suggests, to mock the romance genre and the tale itself.

Not only is the tale a parody of tail-rhyme romances such as *Guy of Warwick* and *Sir Launfal*, but it is also told by the narrator-pilgrim, and thus relates to Chaucer's literary reputation and textual output. This connection is emphasised by the narrator's admission that "oother

---

26 Ann S. Haskell, "Sir Thopas: The Puppet's Puppet", *Chaucer Review* 9 (1975): 253–61.
27 Lee Patterson, "What Man Artow? Authorial Self-Definition in The Tale of Sir Thopas and The Tale of Melibee", *Studies in the Age of Chaucer* 11 (1989): 117–75.
28 *Sir Gawain and the Green Knight*, J. R. R. Tolkien, E. V. Gordon and Norman Davis (eds.), 2nd edn. Oxford: Clarendon Press, 1967.
29 Ruth Waterhouse and Gwen Griffiths, "'Sweete wordes' of Non-Sense: The Deconstruction of the Moral *Melibee* (Part I)", *Chaucer Review* 23 (1989): 338–61.
30 Martin Stevens, "Chaucer's 'Bad Art': The Interrupted Tales", in *The Rhetorical Poetics of the Middle Ages: Reconstructive Polyphony*, John M. Hill and Deborah M. Sinnreich-Levi (eds.). Madison, NJ: Fairleigh Dickinson University Press, 2000: 130–48, at 131.

tale certes kan I noon,/But of a rym I lerned longe agoon" (VII.708–9); if the narrator and Chaucer are conflated, this is ironic false modesty on Chaucer's part, because he obviously can produce many other tales, and has been doing so for the better part of a quarter century, as the Man of Law laments.

Thopas's failure demands that an alternative take its place. *Melibee* is the most obvious candidate, since it is presented as a replacement. But if *Thopas* is a parody of romance, another, more implicit alternative comes to the fore – namely, Chaucer's less parodic romances, such as the *Knight's Tale* and *Troilus and Criseyde*. If we compare the narrator's and Chaucer's attempts at romance, other differences come to light beside the obvious ones of tone and plot that facilitate the parody of *Thopas*. *Troilus and Criseyde* focuses on the knight as lover, as do the *Book of the Duchess* and the *Knight's Tale*. In *Troilus and Criseyde* we find that Chaucer is aware of his preference:

> And if I hadde ytaken for to write
> The armes of this ilke worthi man,
> Than wolde ich of his batailles endite;
> But for that I to writen first began
> Of his love, I have seyd as I kan –
> His worthi dedes, whoso list hem heere,
> Rede Dares, he kan telle hem alle ifeere. (V.1765–71)

Thopas, however, focuses on the knight as warrior, and the martial aspects of the poem have echoes in other so-called popular romances such as *Guy of Warwick*, *Lybeaus Desconus*, and *Sir Launfal*, which, despite a love-element, foreground a martial dimension to the plot.

It would appear from this brief overview that Chaucer does not reject the entire romance tradition – only its martial trappings. This is perhaps because Chaucer had little interest in heroism. J. A. Burrow suggests that Ricardian poetry as he defines it – i.e., the works of Chaucer, Gower, Langland and the *Pearl*-poet – is emphatically non-heroic.[31] Burrow notes that

---

31   J. A. Burrow, *Ricardian Poetry*. London: Routledge, 1971: Ch.3.

whereas in *Beowulf* the genealogical prologue of the Danish kings serves to introduce a hero who, both by his rank and by the historic (or pseudo-historic) significance of his battles, himself deserves to stand beside Scyld, Heremod and the other "þeodcyningas", the corresponding prologue in *Gawain* introduces an adventure which has no significance at all for the history of the kings of Britain.[32]

Similarly, Chaucer's poetry contains for Burrow "a pervasive sense of the unheroic, latterday character of contemporary realities"[33] where the epic world of great beginnings and endings (to use Burrow's phrase) finds no place. Burrow argues that the

> figure of Chaucer's Troilus illustrates how even the most eligible Ricardian hero can fall short of epic stature. Troilus lives in a great age of "beginnings and endings", the era of the siege of Troy; and as one of the sons of King Priam, he plays a prominent part in the defence of the city. ... Yet his "adventures in loving" have even less public consequence than Gawain's Adventure of the Green Chapel.[34]

This Ricardian ethos is markedly different from the concerns of the tail-rhyme romances which Chaucer parodies in the *Tale of Sir Thopas*, and from this perspective a picture of two disparate cultures emerges. If he is not mocking the entertainment of the lower-classes, he is at least mocking a literature which, as far as he is concerned, lacks the introspective human concern that he and Gower can offer. The different literary traditions of popular romance and canonical Ricardian literature are thus defined and separated, resulting in a distinction that survives to this day.[35]

If its martial aspects distance *Thopas* from the idea of man we find in Ricardian poetry, its analytical vapidity distances it from its replacement, the *Melibee*, which is presented from the start as a moral treatise. The significance of *Melibee* is only now beginning to be appreciated, despite (or perhaps because of) its complex ideological frame-

---

32 Ibid., 95–6.
33 Ibid., 97.
34 Ibid., 99.
35 See, for example, Nicola MacDonald, *Pulp Fictions of Medieval England: Essays in Popular Romance*. Manchester: Manchester University Press, 2004.

work. *Melibee* is an attempt to construct a literary community that must exchange ideas and share a communal experience of both literate and oral discourse that will help them to thrive ethically and intellectually. Without the free interchange of ideas and debate on proper behaviour, a culture will become blinded by base emotions and have its dignity and prudence replaced with blind vengeance and rage in an eternal cycle of the sort of violence we find glorified by the martial tail-rhyme romances. I would like to demonstrate this aspect of the tale by examining how one of its stylistic features relates to the debate between Melibee and Prudence on the question of how to respond to injustice and violent provocation.

Some scholars have found in the ironic juxtaposition of *Thopas* and *Melibee* a distinction between the oral and literate worlds of storytelling. Seth Lerer suggests that the literate texture of *Melibee* is central to its relationship to *Thopas*, which he believes represents a "romance of orality"; I understand this to mean an inferior, childlike mode of transmission, to which *Melibee* is a more sophisticated antidote, a work of literateness the textuality of which is "to be linked to sober understanding, rational discussion, and reflective civic duty".[36] I would like to suggest that *Melibee* itself puts such a binary opposition in doubt because it disregards a schism between oral and literate communication, and it embodies the spirit of publicly performed and interpreted literature; in my view, the style of the *Melibee* combines with its content – the debate on revenge versus forgiveness – to invite a communal response. Joyce Coleman suggests that "medieval readers chose to share their experience of literature because they valued shared experience";[37] *Melibee*, despite its lacklustre modern reception, was written for an audience of late fourteenth century men and women who would have seen in Melibee's and Prudence's discourse fertile ground for a public debate on justice, vengeance, and Christian forgiveness.

36 Seth Lerer, "'Now Holde youre mouth': The Romance of Orality in the *Thopas-Melibee* Section of the *Canterbury Tales*", in *Oral Poetics in Middle English Poetry*, Mark Amodio (ed.). New York: Garland, 1994: 181–205, at 184.
37 Joyce Coleman, *Public Reading and the Reading Public in Late Medieval England and France*. Cambridge: Cambridge University Press, 1996: 221.

From beginning to end, *Melibee* is dedicated to citing oral discourse such as proverbs, sermons, and debates, as well as texts which are themselves mixtures of oral and literate communication, most notably the Bible. Of particular interest are the proverbs, to which Chaucer draws attention in the narrator-pilgrim's introduction to the tale: "I telle somwhat moore/Of proverbes than ye han herd bifoore" (VII.955–6). In Chaucer's era and before, proverbs were seen as bits of wisdom that could be drawn from memory to apply to appropriate circumstances. In medieval universities, Latin proverbs were recited by students until they were memorised – then they could be retrieved at the appropriate moment by the student and applied to a context, oral or written, where their contained wisdom was relevant. These Latin proverbs were collected and preserved in text form in long lists, not to be read silently in private, but as a reference for oral recitation. In this context, the proverb encapsulates the complex oral/literate landscape typical of the Middle Ages: often transmitted by speech, proverbs were put in writing to be preserved and to be read aloud amongst a community that could use them as a frame of reference and point of departure in discussions and debates. Proverbs became a textual genre alongside an oral discourse with which they often intersected. Betsy Bowden argues that *Melibee* can be considered a proverb collection – a genre of text which had been used in educational settings as a means of training the memory and transmitting wisdom from generation to generation.[38] In his presentation of the text, then, Chaucer does not effect a world of

---

38 "Within Chaucer's sociohistorical context, a proverb collection could function as a vehicle to convey basic literacy, religious instruction, courtly manners, political allegory, political advice, patristic exegesis, and other concepts according to which scholars have analyzed the *Tale of Melibee*" (Betsy Bowden, "Ubiquitous Format? What Ubiquitous Format? Chaucer's *Tale of Melibee* as a Proverb Collection", *Oral Tradition* 17 (2002): 169–207, at 174). See also Ernst Robert Curtius, *European Literature and the Latin Middle Ages*, Willard R. Trask (trans.). New York, NY.: Harper & Row, 1953: 57–61. Cameron Louis, "The Concept of the Proverb in Middle English", *Proverbium* 14 (1997): 173–85, and A. J. Minnis, *Medieval Theory of Authorship: Scholastic Literary Attitudes in the Later Middle Ages*, 2nd edn. Aldershot: Scolar Press, 1988: 9–12. The political implications of *Melibee* have been explored by David Wallace, *Chaucerian Polity*. Stanford, Calif.: Stanford University Press, 1997: Ch.8.

pure literate culture removed from *Thopas*; he evokes a genre both popular and academic which is not limited to a context of erudite literate transmission and reception, but it is not entirely oral, either.

If we examine Chaucer's evocation of proverbs in full, the intersection of oral and literate communication that permeated Chaucer's world becomes apparent:

> If that yow thynke I varie as in my speche,
> As thus, though that I telle somwhat moore
> Of proverbes than ye han herd bifoore
> Comprehended in this litel tretys heere,
> To enforce with th'effect of my mateere;
> And thogh I nat the same wordes seye
> As ye han herd, yet to yow alle I preye
> Blameth me nat, for, as in my sentence,
> Shul ye nowher fynden difference
> Fro the sentence of this tretys lyte
> After the which this murye tale I write. (VII.954–64)

The narrator begins by referring to his speech, which he will give with more proverbs than his audience has heard before. He again apologises for not *saying* the same words as they have *heard*. Then, curiously, he ends by referring to the tale that he has written. Within the fiction of the *Canterbury Tales*, the narrator's address to a hearing audience makes perfect sense, while his reference to writing does not; like the famous request that readers "Turne over the leef and chese another tale" (I.3177), here we find the fiction of the *Canterbury Tales* interrupted and the voice of the "narrator" disappearing to expose the voice of Chaucer, addressing his real audience with apology. Thus the "ye" of VII.962 is Chaucer's real audience, the actual human beings who read, or heard, the *Canterbury Tales*. Whether the "yow" of VII.954 is also Chaucer's real audience can be debated, but it would not be surprising if many of Chaucer's contemporaries identified themselves with that address in retrospect after coming across the "write" at the end of this sentence.

Just as Chaucer's presentation of *Melibee* brings to mind the oral world of folk wisdom, so the treatise's style consistently reminds readers of the natural patterns of speech. Chaucer repeatedly employed what Anne Herlyn calls "multiple dialogue introducers" (MDIs), which she defines as the repeated use of a verb (answer, ask, say, etc.) in the introduction of direct speech.[39] These often occur in present-day oral storytelling in English, such as: "So he says to her, he says, 'Well,' he says, 'The person at thirty-four backed out'".[40] Multiple dialogue introducers take on two syntactic forms: coordinated (that is, when two different verbs are used) and asyndetic, or when the same verb is repeated.[41] In *Melibee*, we find both forms:

> This Melibeus answerede anon and seyde, "What man," quod he, "shoulde of his wepyng stente that hath so greet a cause for to wepe?" (VII.986)

> For Senec seith thus: "That maister," he seith, "is good that proveth shrewes." (VII.1437)

The first instance, which is an example of the coordinated form, is in the narrator's voice, while the second is a quotation from Prudence.

Prudence uses multiple dialogue introducers eleven times.[42] Her use of the form can be considered Chaucer's mimetic representation of speech in the fiction of the tale. Long ago, Margaret Schlauch argued that "the discussion [between Melibee and Prudence] sounds a bit more like a real conversation than it did in the original" by virtue of the characters' heightened use of vocatives, hedging and conversational adverbials;[43] I would add that Prudence's use of the MDIs

---

39   Anne Herlyn, "So He Says to Her, He Says, 'Well,' He Says…: Multiple Dialogue Introducers From a Historical Perspective", in *Historical Discourse Analysis*, Andreas H. Jucker et al. (eds.). Amsterdam: John Benjamins, 1999: 313–30, at 313.
40   Nessa Wolfson, *CHP: The Conversational Historical Present in American English Narrative*. Dordrecht: Foris, 1982: 26, taken by Herlyn for the title of her article.
41   Herlyn, "So He Says To Her", 313–17.
42   At VII.991, 1185, 1437, 1502–3, 1509–10, 1556, 1602–3, 1621, 1639, and 1660–1.
43   Margaret Schlauch, "The Art of Chaucer's Prose", in *Chaucer and Chaucerians: Critical Studies in Middle English Literature*, D. S. Brewer (ed.). London: Thomas Nelson and Sons, 1966: 140–63.

makes the conversation seem more realistic, and emphasises the colloquial nature of the discourse.

However, the significance of the MDIs is not limited to a mimetic representation of speech within the story. The narrator also uses these forms a total of nineteen times;[44] in three of these instances (at VIII.1236–9, 1283–5, and 1735–41), the second dialogue introducer is separated from the first by a significant block of text, while in the vast majority of instances they are separated only by a single word or clause. It is significant that these stylistic features are almost entirely Chaucer's additions. Of the twenty-nine MDIs I have found in the tale, only six are to be found in Chaucer's source text – Renaud de Louens's French translation of Albertano de Brescia's *Liber consolationis et consilii*.[45] This leaves twenty-three MDIs – 79% of the total count – which are Chaucerian additions. The result of the repeated use of this grammatical structure is a style which Chaucer consciously employed either to imitate the style of speech, which is of course in line with the overarching fiction of the *Canterbury Tales*, or to acclimate the text for public performance, or both.

I believe that Chaucer's motivations in highlighting the conversational nature of the text go deeper still. Although it is sensible and satisfying to say that *Melibee's* style accommodates future oral performances of the text, Chaucer does not accommodate for the oral mode of textual reception in quite the same way in his other prose works – even when they are addressed to an audience of hearers. In fact, the frequent use of MDIs in the *Tale of Melibee* is exceptional to Chaucer's prose style. We do not find it being employed at all in *Boece*, and I have been able to find only one instance of it in the *Parson's Tale*, which, like *Melibee*, adopts many texts to propound a thesis:

---

44   VII.980, 986, 1001, 1011–12, 1051–2, 1055, 1064, 1232–3, 1236–9, 1265–6, 1283–5, 1335, 1713–14, 1735–42, 1779–80, 1793–4, 1808–11, 1816–17, and 1835–6.
45   I am using William Askins's critical edition of Renaud's text in Robert Correale and Mary Hamel, *Sources and Analogues of the Canterbury Tales I*. Cambridge: Boydell and Brewer, 2002: 321–408.

> I seye that somtyme contricioun delivereth a man fro synne;/ of which that David seith, "I seye," quod David (that is to seyn, I purposed fermely) "to shryve me, and thow, Lord, relessedest my synne." (X.308–9)

The emphasis on oral communication within the text does not end here. It is almost entirely a dialogue between Melibee and Prudence, giving it a dramatic feel. Although references to books permeate the tale, the verb "say" is used regularly when accompanying the subject "book" or an author's name; I have found a total of 155 such occurrences. A typical example, which I have already discussed as an example of an MDI, is at VII.1437: "'For Senec seith thus: "That maister," he seith, "is good that proveth shrewes"'". The narrator as well as Prudence, Melibee, and other characters all share this use of the verb, while they use the verbs "write" and "read" to refer to texts much more infrequently – a total of only six times (one instance, at VII.1440, is used in tandem with "seith", rendering its connection to purely literate communication tenuous). Three of these are used by Prudence at the end of the tale (starting at VII.1846) in quick succession in a final attempt to dissuade Melibee from exiling the three "olde foes" who assaulted her and their daughter. Perhaps Prudence effects this change in referential diction as a last ditch effort to win Melibee over. The narrator suggests that Prudence's "wise informaciouns and techynges" help Melibee to "enclyne to the wil of his wif" (VII.1870–1); the textuality of her wise information and teaching bolster her case, and provide her argument with the authority that affirms its veracity.

It is true that these uses of "say" in relation to texts reflect the fact that in Chaucer's English this verb can refer to written communication, as it still can in modern English, but I do not think this renders the diction entirely insignificant. Chaucer's consistent choice of the verb "say" over "write" emphasises the intersections of both communication modalities in a way that compliments the text's dramatic structure and Chaucer's use of a dialogic style in the voices of Prudence and the narrator. Whether Melibee and Prudence read these books privately or aloud to one another, the *Tale of Melibee* can be interpreted as a tale in which books become speech in the debate on action versus patience, rendering an oral/literate division between *Sir Thopas* and *Melibee* strained.

I have already mentioned that Alan Gaylord has suggested *Sir Thopas* is mere *solaas* and the *Melibee* mere *sentence*, and the link between the two is the implication that stories must balance delight with didactics.[46] C. David Benson goes further to suggest that the *Tale of Sir Thopas*'s and the *Tale of Melibee*'s "literary [that is, stylistic] contrast is extreme and total".[47] This idea was also expressed by Tony Davenport, who surely draws upon Gaylord in his recent discussion of the *Thopas-Melibee* link:

> [I]n *Sir Thopas* Chaucer shows by exaggeration where writing only for "solas" can lead; escapism without sense is a logical extreme of the avoidance of serious purpose in narrative. *Melibee* can be seen as the other extreme, "sentence" without much "solas".[48]

Accordingly, the question Chaucer raises with these two works is, to quote Benson again, "Can a poet delight without instructing or instruct without delight? The answer is held within the tales themselves".[49] According to Benson's, Gaylord's and Davenport's readings, Chaucer represents two ways of using language by telling these two tales: the imaginative and the instructive. The instruction the *Melibee* provides is not purely from books, as Chaucer hints at in commenting on his use of proverbial wisdom, and those books themselves do not reflect a world of pure literate thought, since they become speech when Prudence quotes them aloud. Her speeches instruct Chaucer's audience and Melibee, who learns well enough to forgive his foes their trespass. The wisdom of *Melibee*, like its style and presentation, surpasses a distinction between literate and oral worlds which the text itself belies.

If we see *Melibee* as an instructive text on the virtue of prudence, Harry Bailly's response seems all the more wrong because he has not only failed to see the allegorical significance of Prudence and the wis-

---

46 Alan Gaylord, "Sentence and Solaas in Fragment VII of the *Canterbury Tales*: Harry Bailly as Horseback Editor", *PMLA* 82 (1967): 226–35.
47 C. David Benson, "Their Telling Difference: Chaucer the Pilgrim and His Two Contrasting Tales", *Chaucer Review* 18 (1983): 61–76, at 65.
48 Tony Davenport, *Medieval Narrative: An Introduction*. Oxford: Oxford University Press, 2004: 256.
49 "Their Telling Difference", 66.

dom of her arguments, but he has also interpreted the tale as another perspective in the debate on marriage and sex relations. One of the difficulties *Melibee* provides is that it is a dialogue but cannot be understood as a drama. Apart from its very beginning and end, the tale has no narrative and nothing really happens. Characterisation is also subordinate to the debate of the tale. Chaucer does not create a stylistic distinction between Prudence's and Melibee's voices: the direct speech of both characters retains the *style clergial*, the chancellery style of the Middle Ages which developed out of Latin and, as Diane Bornstein notes, is characterised

> by the use of formulaic expressions, terms of reference..., introductory phrases, Latinate words, elaborate explanations, legal phrases, synonyms (particularly doublets), reliance on the passive voice, and a grave, ceremonious tone.[50]

Chaucer adapted this style from Louens and modified it in many ways, such as by adding MDIs, to encourage a communal response. I have only studied one of many features of *Melibee* that invite debate and public mediation. Karla Taylor recently studied how Chaucer's use of doublets in *Melibee* help him to "create a civil society by means of language" by providing the linguistic alternatives of various aspects of English society.[51] Josephine W. Bennett's observation that *Melibee* represents a legal process in which antagonistic parties confronted one another to reach a resolution (called the accord or "loveday")[52] again suggests that *Melibee* produces a literary community of individuals who are united by their appreciation of the text and its greater implications.

Harry Bailly's misunderstanding of Chaucer's text is a stark contrast to this response. Chaucer and his audience can laugh at Harry's domestic interpretation while they can chuckle at this henpecked and

---

50 Diane Bornstein "Chaucer's *Tale of Melibee* as an Example of the *Style Clergial*", *Chaucer Review* 12 (1978): 236–54, at 237.
51 Karla Taylor, "Social Aesthetics and the Emergence of Civic Discourse from the *Shipman's Tale* to *Melibee*", *Chaucer Review* 39 (2005): 298–322, at 316.
52 See especially Ian Rowney, "Arbitration in Gentry Disputes of the Later Middle Ages", *History* 67 (1982): 367–74, at 370 and Josephine W. Bennett, "The Mediaeval Loveday", *Speculum* 33 (1958): 351–70.

defeated husband, and they can at least feel that they have understood something more significant about the text's implications for public policy and justice. Here we find Harry playing the part often reserved for Chaucer's narrator; he is an outsider to the textual community implied and created by Chaucer's textual output. Perhaps this is why Harry moves away from the debate of the tale (which he never acknowledges) to tell an anecdote about his wife. Even if Chaucer's audience's reactions differ, their resulting discussion implies that they have, unlike Harry, taken the core argument of *Melibee* to heart: one must debate and consider before acting on or rejecting advice and ideas.

Chaucer also invites his audience to see a contrast between *Melibee* and *Thopas*. An understanding of this juxtaposition in terms of genre, authorial intention, and the texts' inherent functions and authority uncover how these two works present alternative textual modes of creating literary communities, and also confirm the superiority of communal response and a public literature. Chaucer presents himself in these two texts, not as an author for hearers versus himself as an author for readers, but as an author who can provide either mere entertainment or texts for public mediation, thereby producing for an audience already familiar with his literary tradition and status a distinction between high intellectualism and popular debasement, with the former ultimately beyond the reach of the likes of Harry Bailly. This sense of superiority towards the Host and his ilk is unabashed snobbery when we consider that Chaucer was writing for social classes far above Harry's station, but it is also positively flattering towards his intended audience, who, by virtue of their hermeneutic sophistication, can confirm the legitimacy of their higher social status. In this sense, Bailly takes on the role of whipping-boy previously shouldered by Chaucer in the *Book of the Duchess*, the *Parliament of Fowls*, and, to a lesser degree, in the *House of Fame*. Chaucer's reassignment of this function in the *Canterbury Tales* represents a significant change in his strategy of self-representation, and prepares us to see in some of his other works an affirmation of textual authority.

Chapter 6
Chaucer's Authority

The Border Between Reputation and Repentance

Chaucer's representation of himself as an author often seems to focus on his position within secular literary canons and in a contemporary society in which his status was, in certain respects, ambiguous and malleable. While his reputation today is largely based on his status as the first grand master of secular narrative in English, his corpus includes religious texts that tell a different story of his sense of himself as an author, largely because they lack the ironic play and secular humanism of texts like *Troilus and Criseyde* and the *Book of the Duchess*. They also demonstrate Chaucer's conscious adaptation of a different social role: that of the appropriator and transmitter of canonical religious sentiment to a vernacular English audience. *Boece* is a clear example of this at work, but to find Chaucer's self-representation as a writer of holy works we must turn to two later texts: the *Second Nun's Tale* and the *Retraction*.

Much has been made of the *Retraction*'s pious (or, for some, sententious) tone. Victor Haines has suggested that Chaucer repents his ubiquitous use of irony because it might lead some readers to sin if they misconstrue it.[1] Close to this argument is Edmund Reiss's reading of the relationship between the *Retraction* and the ironic *Canterbury Tales*, which necessitates contrition and penance.[2] Without a renunciation of his secular texts, Reiss believes, Chaucer cannot move the text outside the realm of art (which in an Augustinian world-view is an inherently flawed representation of reality) towards Truth. We do

---

1 "Where are Chaucer's 'Retracciouns'?" *Florilegium* 10 (1988–91): 127–49.
2 See "Chaucer and Medieval Irony", *Studies in the Age of Chaucer* 1 (1979): 67–82.

not see a rhetorical stance taken solely in this proclamation; instead, Chaucer's status as a writer is the context that introduces the rhetoric of the *Retraction*, which I believe emphasises the religious culture shared by Chaucer and his audience. Here Chaucer does not appear to be mediating his social position and defining his literary status; rather, he is a Christian who has written some sinful texts and who must reconcile his textual output with his hopes for a re-unification with God.

The Augustinian dialectic between the worlds of the artificial and the natural is central to this interpretation. For present-day secular readers who do not hold this perspective, the *Retraction* can be problematic and unsympathetic because it seems to deny lasting validity in any secular human experience or creativity that cannot be reconciled with Christian faith. Christian *contemptus mundi* is not unfamiliar to Chaucer, who concludes *Troilus and Criseyde* with a similar ethos. In the *Retraction*, he finally chooses the highest good – that is, hope for an ascent to the heavenly sphere where he has left Troilus. Divine love replaces worldly love, which, as transient and unstable, can all too easily gravitate toward sin.[3]

Although the *Retraction* is clearly directed toward God, it is explicitly addressed to an audience of "hem alle that herkne this litel tretys or rede" (X.1081). The incongruence between addressed and intended audience is, I think, significant; this is not a formal confession, it is not a prayer, and, whether or not Chaucer wrote it on his deathbed, it still speaks with the voice of a secular poet to a human audience, who are asked to "preye for me that Crist have mercy on me and foryeve me my giltes" (X.1084). While his individual textual contributions are put under scrutiny, an Augustinian sublimation of the self beneath universal Christian faith puts Chaucer closer to proper piety and justifies the energies he has spent on crafting moral texts while taking responsibility and expressing regret for his sinful literary activities.

---

3 Joseph Gallagher also found this to be a central theme of the *Second Nun's Tale* – see "Theology and Intention in Chaucer's *Troilus*", *Chaucer Review* 7 (1972): 44–66.

This religious focus is underscored by a subtle shift of identification; instead of defining his audience as separate from and unlike himself, Chaucer here unites himself to them. When he thanks Jesus Christ and Mary, he combines the first person singular with the first person *plural* pronoun: "thanke I oure Lord Jhesu Crist and his blisful Mooder, and alle the seintes of hevene" (X.1089). For an audience familiar with Chaucer and his style, this second person plural is startling. Throughout the dream visions, *Troilus and Criseyde*, and the *Canterbury Tales*, he emphasises the yawning gap between him and those he addresses; they are of different worlds, and at every turn he hints that he is not a part of the secular community which both his own and other literary works help to create. The *Retraction* tells us that if he is removed from his audience in the world of secular love, he is nevertheless united to them in faith. Here social structures begin to break down because Jesus is "kyng of kynges and preest over alle preestes, that boghte us with the precious blood of his herte" (X.1091). Much has changed since the Servant of the Servants of Love addressed "ye loveres" in *Troilus and Criseyde*, or since Chaucer's narrator held his hat awkwardly before the grieving Black Knight in *Book of the Duchess*.

For Chaucer and his contemporaries, all goodness naturally had its source in the Godhead, and it is this source which he credits for any good work he has done: "if ther be any thyng in it [this *litel tretys*] that liketh hem, that therof they thanken oure Lord Jhesu Crist, of whom procedeth al wit and al goodnesse" (X.1081). Here he uses the rhetorical commonplace of moving credit for good poetry to express his spiritual obedience. At the same time, he accepts responsibility for his textual sins:

> Wherfore I biseke yow mekely, for the mercy of God, that ye preye for me that Crist have mercy on me and foryeve me my giltes; and namely of my translacions and enditynges of worldly vanitees, the whiche I revoke in my retracciouns: as is the book of Troilus; the book also of Fame; the book of the XXV. Ladies; the book of the Duchesse; the book of Seint Valentynes day of the Parlement of Briddes; the tales of Caunterbury, thilke that sownen into synne; the book of the Leoun; and many another book, if they were in my remembrance, and many a song and many a leccherous lay, that Crist for his grete mercy foryeve me the synne. (X.1084–7)

We have seen how the catalogue in the *Man of Law's Prologue* assumes a shared knowledge of Chaucer's literary status, and, like the authority-defying narrator of the *House of Fame*, it challenges the singular canonicity of ancient authors. Similarly, in the *Prologue* to the *Legend of Good Women* Chaucer's moral failures are textual because his status as an author is absolute, and his failures are to be taken as seriously as they can within the playful game of love. In the *Retraction*, the catalogue has a resolutely more serious tone because here Chaucer is negotiating the fate of his immortal soul. To do this, he must carefully present a catalogue of his texts and admit and repent their sins, which is only possible if he identifies himself as a writer of immoral secularity. In his penance, Chaucer implies his established status as an author.

Not all of his writings are sinful, however, and Chaucer the Christian selects a few of his works with which he is content:

> But of the translacion of Boece de Consolacione, and othere bookes of legends of seintes, and omelies, and moralitee, and devocioun, that thanke I oure Lord Jhesu Crist and his blissful Mooder, and alle the seintes of hevene, bisekynge hem that they from hennes forth unto my lyves ende sende me grace to biwayle my giltes and to studie to the salvacioun of my soule, and graunte me grace of verray penitence, confessioun and satisfaccioun to doon in this present lyf (X.1088–90)

This passage identifies a unique and important social function that he and his writing perform: to translate moral and devout texts for a vernacular audience and to provide them with the religious sentence so lacking from his other works.

Without records of audience responses contemporaneous with Chaucer, we can never know whether late fourteenth century readers accepted this distinction. If fifteenth century readers are anything to go by, it seems that Chaucer's warnings about his "translacions and enditynges of worldly vanitees" were not heeded. In the first book of the *Fall of Princes* John Lydgate presents with reverence a catalogue of Chaucer's canon, including the "sinful" works,[4] and Robert Henry-

---

4   For a discussion of this reference, see Seth Lerer, *Chaucer and His Readers*. Princeton, NJ: University Press, 1993: 86–7.

son praises "worthie Chaucer glorious" (*Testament* 41), who wrote "In gudelie termis, and in ioly veirs" of Troilus's suffering (*Testament* 59). As I mention in Chapter 1, praise of Chaucer's rhetorical gifts soon became a commonplace. The anonymous writer of the *Book of Curtesye*, who urges his youthful audience to read Chaucer's works, never considers the potential immorality of Chaucer's books, just as he tells his young reader to read everything written by Chaucer ("Redeth my chylde redeth his bookes alle", 351). While fifteenth century followers of Chaucer devoted their energy to reading, canonising, and expanding his poetry after his death, they did not echo his caveat about its sinfulness. Perhaps Chaucer would have found it ironic, or even dangerous, that later generations would devote so much energy to his "bad" works when they should be focusing on the "good". If the *Retraction*'s implicit instructions to ignore Chaucer's sinful texts were followed by future generations, the human comedy, ironic gameplay, and secular interest of his works would have been rejected and possibly lost.

However, to judge Chaucer by a modern, secular appreciation for the non-religious is unfair and anachronistic. We cannot expect a fourteenth century English bureaucrat to perceive a future conflict between religious sentiments and a more secular value-system – especially if such a distinction could not exist in the culture of the era. Nor, it must be said, did Chaucer imagine himself as having a non-Christian readership. Although the community envisioned by the *Retraction* can seem unnecessarily exclusive to us today, in Chaucer's own time and society it was inclusive, since he was not writing for non-Christians. His use of the first person plural pronoun underlines a unity between himself and his audience that is emphatically absent in most of his other writings. If we accept that the *Retraction* lacks irony and is directed towards God, then this authorial self-representation is an earnest acknowledgment of, and regret for, his sinful secular writings. His identification of himself as a transmitter of religious works is the opposite side of the same coin: in those texts his social function as a writer is virtuous and significant. Within the Christian context behind the *Retraction*, Chaucer is united to his audience by virtue of his holy works because their religion ultimately unites all believers in a single community of faith.

If Chaucer contrasts the worlds of secular entertainment and moral instruction in the narrator-pilgrim's two tales, he contemplates this contrast in the final word on his literary career in the *Retraction*. Like the *Man of Law's Prologue* and the *Prologue* to the *Legend of Good Women*, the *Retraction* focuses on himself as a writer for an English community. However, this is where the similarities more or less cease; in the *Retraction*, Chaucer takes seriously his literary status and the socio-religious ethics of vernacular writing, and does not take the opportunity to make a self-deprecating joke or to mediate his social relationships or literary reputation. Instead, the text concerns itself with God's judgment for Chaucer's textual sins, and the sinful narratives are, in Larry Scanlon's words, "an integral part of the narrative logic" that leads up to the *Retraction*.[5] The *Retraction* gives us an insight into Chaucer as a medieval Christian, preparing himself for contrition, death, and the re-unification with God that will hopefully follow. In doing so, he pronounces a judgment on his own poetry – a move which is, for him and his era, a spiritual and ideological necessity but which to many today is likely to seem very alien and destructively fundamentalist.

---

[5] Larry Scanlon, *Narrative, Authority and Power: The Medieval Exemplum and the Chaucerian Tradition*, Cambridge: Cambridge University Press, 1994: 24. Scanlon extends this reading further to suggest that the sinful works here are not so much rejected as consolidated, because without them there is no logic in Chaucer's retractions. However, consider the more widely accepted position expressed by Gregory Roper, "Dropping the Personae and Reforming the Self: The *Parson's Tale* and the End of the *Canterbury Tales*", in *Closure in the Canterbury Tales: The Role of the Parson's Tale*, David Raybin and Linda Tarte Holley (eds.). Kalamazoo, Mich.: Western Michigan University Press, 2000: 151–75, who understands Chaucer's discarding of his sinful self in the *Retraction* as an effort to rediscover his true self as a human *imago Dei*. See also Stephen Knight's study of the relationship between the *Retraction* and the *Parson's Tale*, which prepares author and reader for an act of penance (see *Geoffrey Chaucer*. Oxford: Blackwell, 1986: 156).

Translating Piety and Textual Transmission in the
Second Nun's Tale

Not everything Chaucer wrote was secular and sinful. Besides the "translacion of Boece de Consolacione" there are the "othere bookes of legendes of seintes, and omelies, and moralitee, and devocioun" that Chaucer wrote throughout his life. While the *Parson's Tale* and the *Man of Law's Tale* most immediately spring to mind, the short hagiography that Chaucer calls the "lyf of Seynt Cecile" in the *Legend of Good Women* (F.426 and G.416) is another example of such a pious text. At some point before 1386–7, this tale existed as a whole unto itself, but it has only survived as the *Second Nun's Tale*. What the *lyf* was like in its original form we can only speculate. Yet certain inconsistencies in the narrative voice of the prologue might indicate that Chaucer changed very little. At lines VIII.62–3, the narrator (who, in accordance with the fiction of the *Canterbury Tales*, should be the Second Nun) states: "And though that I, unworthy sone of Eve,/Be synful, yet accepte my bileve". The apparent change of the speaker's sex may be jarring to modern readers, who expect a consistent narrative fiction throughout a literary text. But for Chaucer the inconsistency was either irrelevant or simply one of the things that he never got around to correcting.[6]

Perhaps this is proof positive that what we have is in fact the *Legend of Saint Cecilia* in an unmodified form. It is unlikely, at any

---

6   On this passage and similar "errors" in the *Canterbury Tales*, Joyce Coleman suggests: "As psychologists and linguists know, it is often a speaker's 'mistakes' that offer the most telling evidence of underlying structures. As a characteristic mistake within the aural-narrative constellation, the ascription of writing to oral narrators or of textualized experience to oral narratees suggests the fundamental aurality of the process. Creating a fictional situation involving a speaker narrating to listeners, that is, authors have trouble keeping it separate from the 'real-world' event of a writer writing a book that will be read aloud to a listening audience. They are liable to think of the oral narrator as writing, and to describe the in-frame oral audience as 'hearing read' or 'hearing above'" (*Public Reading and the Reading Public in Late Medieval England and France*. Cambridge: Cambridge University Press, 1996: 105–6).

rate, that only this line was carried over from the original, and the inconsistent narrative voice can be taken to indicate that the saint's life was added at some point to the *Canterbury Tales*. The masculine "sone" of the *Invocacio* makes it obvious that this is not the voice of the Second Nun, who, as William Quinn notes, "is never described, she is never even named."[7] Such a theory becomes more tantalising when we consider that Chaucer calls the *Second Nun's Tale* "the lyf of Seinte Cecile" in the *Prologue* to the *Canon's Yeoman's Tale* (VIII.554). As Ralph Hanna notes, the "only real anomaly in the *a* order [i.e. the Ellesmere I–X order of the *Canterbury Tales* used in the *Riverside*] is the position of Fragment VIII [which contains the *Second Nun's Tale* and the *Canon's Yeoman's Tale*]".[8] One of the difficulties in establishing this tale's position in the *Canterbury Tales* is that of identifying thematic or narrative links with the texts to which it is joined.[9] Its relationship to the *Canon's Yeoman's Tale* has been appraised by a number of scholars,[10] but although the two have some

---

7 William Quinn notes the futility of the Chaucerian's predisposition to hunt for irony in the *Second Nun's Tale*: "Though I myself have tried, out of habit, to hear the familiarly ironic voice of Chaucer in the Second Nun's tale, I see no reason to doubt that her simply pious voice was once the poet's own as well. The tale's own prologue makes such doubts dubious," *Chaucer's* Rehersynges: *The Performability of* The Legend of Good Women, Washington, D.C.: University Press of America, 1994: 215. Joseph L. Grossi Jr., "The Unhidden Piety of Chaucer's *Seint Cecilie*," *The Chaucer Review* 36 (2002): 298–309 states plainly that "Chaucer too took seriously the religious vision of this work" (299).

8 *Riverside Chaucer*, 1121.

9 However, consider Eric Weil's argument for a connection between Fragments VIII and IX on the basis that they oppose each other in the images of sight and blindness, idleness versus work, and alchemical transformation – see "An Alchemical Freedom Flight: Linking the Manciple's Tale to the Second Nun's and Canon's Yeoman's Tales", *Medieval Perspectives* 6 (1990): 162–70. Stephen Knight also suggests that the "Second Nun's tale asserts straight, orthodox Christianity after the Nun's Priest has dismissed all other late medieval cultural practices" (*Geoffrey Chaucer*, 145), thus framing the *Second Nun's Tale* and the *Nun's Priest's Tale* in a debate about proper methods of piety.

10 See, for example, Joseph Grennen, "Saint Cecilia's 'Chemical Wedding': The Unity of the Canterbury Tales, Fragment VIII", *Journal of English and Germanic Philology* 65 (1966): 466–81; Russell A. Peck, "The Ideas of 'Entente' and Translation in Chaucer's *Second Nun's Tale*", *Studia Mediaevale* 8 (1967):

thematic similarities, a narrative or generic connection between them never emerges; as Robert Longsworth observes, the *Second Nun's Tale* is presented as a translation, whereas the *Canon's Yeoman's Tale* is presented as the Canon's Yeoman's full confession.[11] Also, the Second Nun is not a described character, and the Canon and his Yeoman are not even pilgrims in the *General Prologue*, which could suggest that both of these tales were not part of Chaucer's original plan (unless the later chance meeting with the Canon and his Yeoman had been Chaucer's intention all along).

Whether because the *Second Nun's Tale* was inserted into the *Canterbury Tales* framework without revision or because Chaucer was more interested in addressing Mary than in creating a unified fictional whole, he speaks as the narrator in the *Invocacio ad Mariam*, and we must consider the invocation as his own, and not the Second Nun's. Its tone is intimate. Chaucer addresses Mary with the second-person singular pronoun, and does not mention his earthly audience until he has completed the invocation, when there is a shift of focus to them:

> Yet preye I yow that reden that I write,
> Foryeve me that I do no diligence
> This ilke storie subtilly to endite,
> For bothe have I the wordes and sentence
> Of hym that at the seintes reverence
> The storie wroot, and folwen hire legende,
> And pray yow that ye wole my werk amende. (VIII.78–84)

In contrast to his address to Mary, Chaucer addresses his readers with the pronoun "yow", which can be read either as a polite or plural des-

---

17–37; Bruce A. Rosenberg, "The Contrary Tales of the Second Nun and the Canon's Yeoman", *Chaucer Review* 2 (1968): 278–91; Glending Olson, "Chaucer, Dante and the Structure of Fragment VIII (G) of the *Canterbury Tales*", *Chaucer Review* 16 (1982): 222–36; Larry Benson "The Aesthetic of Chaucer's Religious Tales in Rhyme Royal", in *Religion in the Poetry and Drama of the Late Middle Ages in England*; and Piero Boitani and Anna Torti (eds.). Cambridge: D. S. Brewer, 1990: 101–17.

11 See Robert Longsworth, "Privileged Knowledge: St. Cecilia and the Alchemist in the *Canterbury Tales*", *Chaucer Review* 27 (1992): 87–96.

ignation. In either case, readers are united by their common task of amending Chaucer's work as a religious community, of which Chaucer is a part by virtue of his faith – a fact made clear in the invocation itself – but from which he is also removed by his differing position in the communicative situation. They are readers, he a writer, and they are given hermeneutic responsibility and authority over Chaucer by virtue of his request for their emendations. This is not to say that he renounces his authorial duties. Nor does he hesitate to exercise his interpretative will, as the first lines of the tale imply:

> First wolde I yow the name of Seint Cecilie
> Expowne, as men may in hir storie see.
> It is to seye in Englissh "hevenes lilie,"
> For pure chaastnesse of virginitee;
> Or, for she whitnesse hadde of honestee,
> And grene of conscience, and of good fame
> The soote savour, "lilie" was hir name. (VIII.85–91)

Chaucer continues to explain the etymology of the name for another 21 lines, where he gives variant translations, while emphasising that each of these are alternatives that he "written fynde" (VIII.94) or which people can choose from ("Men myghte hire wel 'the hevene of peple' calle" VIII.104).

The emphatic relationship between the worlds of words and men is unsurprising in the Aquinian tradition in which, as A. J. Minnis puts it, "God is the sole *auctor* of things and can use things to signify, whereas human *auctores* are *auctores* of words and use words to signify";[12] the relationship, then, between Cecilia (in this sense the thing signified) and her name (the *figura* used) must be expounded to uncover her moral sanctity. This is done both in Chaucer's text and the original by reference to the etymology of her name.[13] The only differ-

---

12   *Medieval Theory of Authorship.* Aldershot: Scolar Press, 1988: 73 and 247n.1. See also *Summa Theologiae* I.1.10, esp. the response and third reply to the objection.
13   This is a method of exposition typical of the Middle Ages – see Ernst R. Curtius, *European Literature and the Latin Middle Ages*. William R. Trask (trans.). New York: Harper & Row, 1953: 497–500 and *Riverside Chaucer*, 944 note to ll.85–119.

ence is that, in Chaucer's version, that etymology extends to English. By Englishing the original etymology, Chaucer here takes seriously his job as a translator and populariser of this foreign tale by domesticating the linguistic exposition in his original. This exercise of the writer's power to mold the text's meaning requires an establishment of authority, so it is unsurprising that we find a prologue to the text between the Marian invocation and the translation proper that makes recourse to "hym that at the seintes reverence/The storie wroot, and [I] folwen hire legende" (VIII.82–3).

This is the self-consciousness of medieval compilers and translators, who often identify their inferior position within the communicative situation and divide authority over the text's meaning and accuracy between the author and reader. A. J. Minnis notes that Chaucer's authorial strategy in general was "to assume the role of compiler and to exploit the literary form of *compilatio*" in a rhetorical game. To quote Minnis further:

> so deliberate was he [Chaucer] in presenting himself as a compiler that one is led to suspect the presence of a very self-conscious author who was concerned to manipulate the conventions of *compilatio* for his own literary ends...Chaucer was an author who hid behind the "shield and defense" of the compiler.[14]

As true as this is for Chaucer's secular texts, in the *Second Nun's Tale* we find him taking on this role seriously and without affectation. Here he is a translator of canonical hagiography, and he addresses his audience in that role without the ironic self-consciousness typical of his many *leccherous lays*.[15] Like *Boece* and the *Parson's Tale*, the *Second Nun's Tale* is the work of Chaucer as a translator who provides a text

---

14 *Medieval Theory of Authorship*, 310.
15 Commonly accepted among Chaucerians is the view that the *Second Nun's Tale* is a pious and non-ironic text. Carolyn Colette notes how the tale's ethical dimension functions to guide men away from earthly desires and towards a spiritual vision – see "A Closer Look at Seinte Cecile's Special Vision", *Chaucer Review* 10 (1976): 337–49. Even the comedy which Anne Eggebroten detected in Chaucer's translation of the tale does not negate its spiritual intention, since comedy is not uncommon in hagiography – see "Laughter in the *Second Nun's Tale*: A Redefinition of the Genre", *Chaucer Review* 19 (1984): 55–61.

not for his audience's entertainment but for their spiritual nourishment.

Chaucer's serious intentions for the *Second Nun's Tale* are also reflected in how he frames the text in relation to his audience. Joyce Coleman finds the tale to be an "anomalous case" because it alone addresses an audience of readers.[16] Yet Coleman does not argue that this address to readers excludes hearers, as Chaucer "often … uses an apparently format-neutral 'read' or else a 'hear' or 'now hearken'" when addressing his audience,[17] and this could appear to be another format-neutral form of the word "read", which is un-weighted in the oral-literate constellation. Because spiritual texts were read aloud in many contexts in the fourteenth century,[18] we cannot argue that the *Second Nun's Tale* is entirely literate because of its genre or religious purpose.

Although clues to the intended modality of the work are not forthcoming, the qualifications of Chaucer's address are highly suggestive. He addresses his audience not as "you hearers and readers", or "you readers", but as "yow that redden that I write". If "read" here is format-neutral, and Chaucer is addressing both hearers and readers, he is still addressing a group that is physically removed from him. If he were to qualify an address to a present audience by singling out those who are paying attention (if we assume that we can translate the phrase to mean "those of you who are listening to me"), this would be a positive affront, backhandedly implying that his audience is actually inattentive, an especially serious lapse in the case of a highly religious text.

Bearing in mind such considerations of tact, the address to the audience, if it does not rule out the possibility of prelection, at least rules out the possibility of auto-prelection. An address to readers and hearers centers the text on both modalities and creates a textual com-

---

16   *Public Reading*, 150.
17   Ibid., 101.
18   See for example the case of Cecily Neville, duchess of York, which is described by Coleman in ibid., 138–40.

munity that includes hearers and readers.[19] We see this strategy in Caxton's addresses to his readership. By referring to readers exclusively, Chaucer offers them the opportunity to feel that the request for textual emendation is addressed to them exclusively – an option hearers do not have.

Chaucer singles out those members of his audience who are reading the text privately to ask them to perform a specifically scholarly and literate act – the emending of the moral failures and errors of his text. This is not to say that this work is intended for solely these literary-professionals, to use Coleman's term.[20] However, this passage as a rhetorical address to readers emphasises the importance and centrality of the scholarly silent readers who were a part of the larger audience awaiting the tale when Chaucer put pen to paper. To them Chaucer assigns the task of interpretation and emendation, much as Gower and Strode are called upon to correct *Troilus and Criseyde*.

Chaucer's emphasis on his readers identifies the text with a larger canon of religious texts. Unlike sermons intended for public delivery, hagiographical writings often focus upon a personal relationship with God to the exclusion of a larger social body. As solemn hagiography written outside the context of the *Canterbury Tales* and not for the voice of an individual fictional character, the *Life of St Cecilia* is a text that must be considered within a context of affective piety and spiritual reverence of the ineffable power of God. For those reading or hearing the text not to amend its errors but to feel God's power, the saint's life is a text that must be accepted on its own terms as an authoritative account of God's mysteries, which are the story's puzzles that readers are invited to solve. The resulting experience of the text is meditative, and its compilers, editors, and translators serve as mediators between God and the spiritual community of its readers and hearers.

Andrew Taylor has observed that, in the Middle Ages, "[f]or many, meditation meant meditative reading", which could take the

---

19 Such a community is implied by the address to readers and hearers at the beginning of the *Retraction*.
20 Ibid., 88–93 *et passim*.

form of being read to as much as it could be silent, private reading.[21] In the early Middle Ages, monks and clerics were the members of a society for whom the reading of texts was a type of worship, and their "motive for reading was ... the salvation of [their] soul".[22] By the later Middle Ages, meditative reading was not only part of the monk's lifestyle; as Brian Stock observes, "[r]eading and meditation, hitherto largely the private preserves of the monastic life, became, by the later twelfth century, general *viatica* to perfection".[23] Meditative reading was not restricted to men; for women, too, reading was a part of devotion and a source of solace.[24] For these texts, the default mode of transmission would have been private reading (if not necessarily silent); Taylor convincingly argues that, in the Middle Ages, "reading ... remained part of a cultural practice in which bookishness, privacy and piety were intimately connected".[25] Instances such as the Nevill household's public readings of religious texts existed alongside a long cultural development of private religious meditation made manifest in social institutions such as anchoritism, the development of the private cell in monasteries, and the iconographic depiction of the scribe copying religious texts in a room alone. More private and more public forms of devotion co-existed – Margery Kempe's priest read to her, and monasteries held public readings of religious texts – but the two are different, if not at odds with each other. In Chaucer's *Second Nun's Tale* what we might be seeing is a rhetorical adaptation of an audience address to make it compatible with both types of religious experience, while affirming the ultimate authority of clerics to mediate the holy text's meaning.

---

21 "Into His Secret Chamber: Reading and Privacy in Late Medieval England" in *The Practice and Representation of Reading in England*, James Raven et al. (eds.). Cambridge: Cambridge University Press, 1996: 41–61, at 44.
22 Parkes, M. B. "Reading, Copying and Interpreting a Text in the Early Middle Ages", in *A History of Reading in the West*, Guglielmo Cavallo and Roger Chartier (eds.). Cambridge: Polity, 1999: 90–102, at 91.
23 "Medieval Literacy, Linguistic Theory, and Social Organization", *NLH* 16 (1984): 13–29, at 19.
24 See discussion in Taylor, 1996: 47–8.
25 Ibid., 48.

Chaucer makes a distinction between different readers and their power to revise the text's meaning because the canonicity of the story disallows a multitude of differing and unique individual responses. It must guide its audience to the unifying truth of God's power and grace, as the *Retraction* sets out to do for Chaucer. An audience of private reader-interpreters temporally and spatially distant from Chaucer as the writer of the work is positioned as mediators of Chaucer's translation of the story to ensure that its canonicity is not corrupted by his alterations (what we might call innovations) to the text. Unlike in *Troilus and Criseyde* and the *Tale of Melibee*, hearers are not invited to feel central to the development of the ongoing project of producing a communal voice, nor can they feel that they are part of the story in the same way as *Troilus and Criseyde*'s audience is invited to; instead, they can only see (or hear) the expression of God's power embodied in the miraculous St Cecilia.

Can we extend this interpretation to *Boece*? Unfortunately, any prologue or epilogue that might originally have been written has since been lost, and what remains is only the translation – which, as Ralph Hanna and Traugott Lawler note, is ambitiously literal.[26] For *Boece* the only insight into Chaucer's strategy as a translator comes from the fact that he translated Boethius' verse into prose – an alteration that Caroline Eckhardt suggests was motivated by a desire to make the text as clear as possible.[27] Similarly, Szilvia Malaczkov argues that Chaucer's translation strategy for *Boece* was to translate content rather than form.[28] The literalness of the text strongly suggests that Chaucer's intention in translating *Boece* was to make available the beneficial instructiveness of Boethius' original text, an act of piety he later stood by in his *Retraction*. The expressed concern for accuracy in the *Second Nun's Tale* finds itself being enacted in *Boece*, where meaning supersedes style. The fact that in these two instances Chaucer extended his social function as a translator/writer of secular texts to the ap-

---

26 See their comments in the *Riverside Chaucer*, 395–7.
27 "The Medieval Prosimetrum Genre (from Boethius to *Boece*)", *Genre* 16 (1983): 21–38.
28 "Geoffrey Chaucer's Translation Strategies", *Perspectives: Studies in Translatology* 9 (2001): 33–44.

propriation of canonical works of religious and philosophical sentiment shows how seriously he took his social function as a translator/compiler for the English. His authority as a translator for the English, however, must be mediated by the authority of his clerical readers, as is to be expected for a fourteenth-century translator. With this caveat, necessitated by the orthodoxies of Christianity at the time, Chaucer was confident in his social function as an importer of continental religious texts and ideas.

Conclusions

The *Second Nun's Tale* shows us Chaucer engaging his God and his audience of readers in a context of intimate religious devotion. Here, the social functions of his other texts are markedly absent, as is Chaucer's otherwise characteristic self-highlighting rhetoric and seemingly modern self-consciousness. Presumably his *Boece* was undertaken within a similar context: to be read as a private religious experience. If his reference to readers existed in the earlier hagiography, which is probable since it makes little sense within the narrative of the *Canterbury Tales*, we cannot suppose that he originally read it aloud to an audience of hearers. Its intended mode of transmission, being readerly (whether private or social), moves Chaucer away from the transmission of the text, and his self-representation as a translator of religious texts both reflects and mediates this distance.

This is not the context we find for the bulk of Chaucer's work, nor for those texts that have won most affection in the minds of readers, either in the century following Chaucer or today. By and large Chaucer represents himself as an earthly writer for a secular audience from which he is socially excluded by his relationships to the world, to books, and to his audience. Throughout most of his works he dehumanises his rhetorical persona so as to humanise his audience. But in the *Second Nun's Tale* he writes much like a diligent translator or compiler of moral sentence. Here he identifies himself as a qualified textual authority who popularises the religious text to give his audience access to it, and his request that silent readers correct his text identifies the various levels of religious authority available to different readers. As religious translations, the *Second Nun's Tale* and *Boece* lack the irony and gameplay of many of Chaucer's other works. In these texts he is conscious of his textual responsibilities, which we find manifested in his literalising translation strategy, audience addresses, and serious approach to the task at hand. Similarly, in the *Retraction* we find Chaucer retreating from his rhetorical narrative persona to address the most important audience of all: God.

What unites the *Retraction* and the *Second Nun's Tale*, and what separates them from the majority of Chaucer's narrative texts, is his non-ironic, non-comical presentation of himself as an established English writer. In contrast to the traditional understanding of Chaucer's narrator as an ironic, comical figure, the *Second Nun's Tale* presents Chaucer speaking through the narrator's voice as a confident translator of religious sentiment. He lays claim to as much authority as a non-clerical writer possibly could in late fourteenth century England, possibly because, by this advanced stage of his life and literary career, he had become an author for the English. Similarly, the *Retraction* focuses on Chaucer as an English writer who must apologise for the unethical elements of his work, and who finds refuge only in those religious texts he has translated and adapted. From a rhetorical perspective, these religious moments are unique in Chaucer's texts because they were not written to mediate Chaucer's social position or to engage in the socio-economic and political landscapes of the day, but rather to express guilt for transcending the boundaries of acceptable Christian writing.

The omission of the self-deprecating persona in the *Second Nun's Tale* shows us that Chaucer ceases to distance himself from communities implied and constructed by his texts when he is in the process of contributing to a religious community which was, for him and his audience members, of absolute importance and by definition universal. The unique first person plural audience address in the *Retraction* is an overt expression of Chaucer's self-identification as a member of the Christian community. When Chaucer evokes this context in his writing, the rhetorical mode of self-representation employed so consistently in his secular texts is suddenly absent. He ceases to play with his social position and those of his readers and hearers, and he no longer implies a textual community from which he is paradoxically excluded. Instead, he addresses a religious community in which he and his audience are united by faith.

Conclusion

Chaucer continually used a narrator persona to position himself vis-à-vis his audience; while they are invited to interpret his works, mediate his meaning, and develop their own moral judgment on the text, he presents himself as a reporter unable and unwilling to provide a monolithic moral attitude or a singular voice. He celebrates plurality and diverse individual opinion, whether on the issue of the formel's choice in the *Parliament of Fowls*, the causes of Troilus' double sorrow, or how Melibee should respond to his foes. He creates for himself the roles of scholarly reader and vernacular writer, and his professed fidelity to texts, authors, and textual discourse distances him from experience of the real world. His perspective, as a result, is subservient to the judgments of his more worldly audience. This may or may not have been the person Chaucer really was, but it is the impression he urges upon his audience.

There are as many possible explanations for this pose as can be imagined, and it would be impossible to argue for any one. The texts preserve Chaucer's rhetorical self-representation, but not his motivations. The impression they give us is that of an affable, warm-hearted, self-deprecating individual, who has an affinity for human beings while being baffled by them. Yet other facets of Chaucer's self-representation belie his self-effacing technique; his bold and independent assertion of authority in the *House of Fame*, his audacious claims to being an English author of poesy in *Troilus and Criseyde*, and his implicit self-praise in the *Tale of Sir Thopas* and the *Tale of Melibee* do not reflect the self-deprecating, humble character often assumed. In these rhetorical moments we find Chaucer's developing confidence in his authorial status, and perhaps even a faint awareness of his future as the father of English poetry.

Chaucer is rarely praised for his consistency, which seems not to have been a great concern for fourteenth century English writers. Yet his self-representation as an asocial bibliophile is surprisingly consistent. From the *Book of the Duchess* to the *Canterbury Tales*, he characterises himself through his narrator as a bookish and irreverent clerk while passing silently over his social and psychological character. His relationship to books develops as he grows increasingly confident with his poetic status, but it remains the primary focus of the narrator's disposition. His audience, however, is rarely characterised by their relationship to books, and often – as in the claims to authority in *Troilus and Criseyde*, the translation of the *Second Nun's Tale*, and the juxtaposition between table games and books in the *Book of the Duchess* – Chaucer emphasises their distance from textual culture and the work of clerks.

His audience's realm is a social one, where public discourse and the shared enjoyment of texts in English produces a community. Their communal experience of literature is celebrated, and the private study of literature is quietly mocked as an asocial and largely fruitless process. In his studies, the narrator fails to learn, no matter how much he tries. Chaucer's audience, by contrast, live in a world where humans interact with each other, share their emotions and ideas, and generally create a culture of ideas and values. Chaucer claims to reflect this culture and to represent it by referring to himself as a writer, and he claims ignorance of its values and complexities by referring to himself as a reader. He becomes a student of the world that he assumes is quotidian for his audience. And like his self-representation, his representation of his audience is a rhetorical move, flattering them with the trappings of courtly culture while implicitly challenging and refining their society, and encouraging them to ask questions of each other.

The distinction that this pose creates is between the audience's communal experience of Chaucer's texts and his narrator's private experience of Chaucer's source-texts. The communities that Chaucer creates by writing can only exist if the individual voices of each person are taken seriously, and he emphasises the value of their voices by refusing, at nearly every turn, to lay claim to dogmatic authority within their society.

From a rhetorical perspective, Chaucer's narratorial self-representation can be described as "co-adaptation", a term used by Roger Sell to define the reciprocal symbiosis that a free exchange of ideas can produce within a community.[1] If the voices of readers are given equal value to the voice of the author, readers can approach the text in an attempt to share and exchange perspectives, gaining not only an understanding of the narrative and its characters, but of differing viewpoints. Chaucer urges such a communal response, and we can only imagine that the initial public reception of his texts, particularly in a circumstance of auto-prelection, would have resulted in a vigorous and excited discussion.

While Chaucer encourages this communal experience of his texts, he presents himself as a silent, solitary reader and an aloof author. Chaucer took and modified this persona largely from the French tradition, in which authors such as Guillaume de Lorris, Jean de Mean, and Guillaume de Machaut presented themselves above all as writers on the periphery of real-world experience. I have remained silent on the Italian tradition, because it does not seem that Dante, Boccaccio, and Petrarch adapted a similar stance, and Chaucer's narrative personae take little from his Italian sources. Like Machaut, Chaucer for the most part represents himself as inferior to the courtly world he is at pains to describe, while he increasingly underscores his own narrative agency and literary significance. His self-deprecation helps him avoid offending his audience – this is most noticeable in *Book of the Duchess*, where his strategy for consoling John of Gaunt is bolstered by a comical characterisation of himself – and it helps him depict himself as a social inferior. At the same time, Chaucer never loses confidence in his clerkliness, and, increasingly, in his authorial status.

This reading is only available to us if we conflate the narrator with Chaucer himself. Although the narrator is a literary fiction, Chaucer invites his audience to see similarities between himself and his construct and, in turn, to conflate them. Thus the narrator of *House of Fame* is named Geffrey, the narrator of *Troilus and Criseyde* is an author, and the narrator of the *Legend of Good Women* has written a

---

[1] In Sell's words, this as the process by which authors "adapt to prevailing social conventions, yet by doing so can also adapt the conventions themselves to his or her more individual perceptions, desires and goals" (*Literature as Communication*. Amsterdam: John Benjamins, 2000: 282).

large number of poems that share titles and plots with Chaucer's own. These narrators are social masks – a way to influence the opinions of others and to maintain a level of distance between audience and speaker. A rhetorical study allows us to see how Chaucer manipulates this distance to create a seeming intimacy between himself and his audience.

The oral mode of reading in Chaucer's era supports such a perspective, while medieval methods of reading and medieval theories of language encourage a perception of texts as representations of authors' voices. With such an understanding of texts and communication, affirmations of authority are easily seen as rhetorically motivated, and it is by rhetoric that the voice of a narrative is constructed – not as a pure fiction, but as a textual representation of the author.

Chaucer takes advantage of this method of reading. He knows that his audience will see in his narrator semblances of Chaucer the man, and he attempts to alter their perceptions of himself by a careful manipulation of his narrator, who is best understood as the author's textual representative. We do not need to be fettered by an obsession with the fallibility of fictional narrators, especially since recent studies suggest that such a way of reading is an anachronistic imposition when applied to the fourteenth century. To read like a modern is to close our ears to Chaucer's rhetorical wit and the relationships his texts had to the men and women for whom they were written. Hopefully, this study has shown that narratives, and the constructs that tell them, do not live in a vacuum, entirely removed from the person who writes them, and that Chaucer's narrator is part of his rhetoric of self-representation.

Bibliography

Adams, Jenny. "Pawn Takes Knight's Queen: Playing with Chess in the *Book of the Duchess*", *Chaucer Review* 34 (1999): 125–38

Aers, David. "The *Parliament of Fowls*: Authority, the Knower and the Known", *Chaucer Review* 16 (1981): 1–17

Alexander, J. J. G. "Painting and Manuscript Illumination for Royal Patrons in the Later Middle Ages", in *English Court Culture in the Later Middle Ages*, V. J. Scattergood and J. W. Sherborne (eds.). London: Duckworth, 1983: 141–62

Allen, Elizabeth. "Chaucer Answers Gower: Constance and the Trouble with Reading", *ELH* 64 (1997): 627–55

Amtower, Laurel. "Authorizing the Reader in Chaucer's *House of Fame*", *Philological Quarterly* 79 (2000): 273–91

Anderson, J. J. "The Narrators in the *Book of the Duchess* and the *Parlement of Foules*", *Chaucer Review* 26 (1992): 219–35

Aristotle. *Rhetoric*, John Henry Freese (ed. and trans.). Cambridge, Mass.: Harvard University Press, 1926

Armitage-Smith, Sydney. *John of Gaunt*. London: Constable and Company, 1904

Augustine of Hippo, *On the Trinity Books 8–15*. Gareth B. Matthews (ed.) and Stephen McKenna (trans.). Cambridge: Cambridge University Press, 2002

Bahr, Arthur W. "The Rhetorical Construction of Narrator and Narrative in Chaucer's the *Book of the Duchess*", *Chaucer Review* 35 (2000): 43–59

Bennett, Josephine W. "The Mediaeval Loveday", *Speculum* 33 (1958): 351–70

Benson, C. David. "Their Telling Difference: Chaucer the Pilgrim and His Two Contrasting Tales", *Chaucer Review* 18 (1983): 61–76

Benson, Larry. "The Aesthetic of Chaucer's Religious Tales in Rhyme Royal", in *Religion in the Poetry and Drama of the*

Late Middle Ages in England, Piero Boitani and Anna Torti (eds.). Cambridge: D. S. Brewer, 1990: 101–17

Benson, Larry D. (ed.). *Riverside Chaucer*, 3rd edn. Boston: Houghton Mifflin, 1987

Bestul, Thomas H. "Chaucer's *Troilus and Criseyde*: The Passionate Epic and its Narrator", *Chaucer Review* 14 (1980): 366–78

Bethurum, Dorothy. "Chaucer's Point of View as Narrator in the Love Poems", *PMLA* 74 (1959): 511–20

Blamires, Alcuin. "A Chaucer Manifesto", *Chaucer Review* 24 (1989): 29–43

Boccaccio, Giovanni. *Il Filostrato,* Nathaniel Edward Griffin and Arthur Beckwith Myrick (eds. and trans.). Philadelphia, Penn.: University of Pennsylvania Press, 1929

Boccaccio, Giovanni. *Il Filostrato*, Vincezo Pernicone (ed.). New York: Garland, 1986

Boitani, Piero. "Old Books Brought to Life in Dreams: The *Book of the Duchess*, the *House of Fame* and the *Parliament of Fowls*", in *The Cambridge Chaucer Companion*, Piero Boitani and Jill Mann (eds.). Cambridge: Cambridge University Press, 1986: 39–57

Bolens, Gullemette. "Chess, Clocks, and Counsellors in Chaucer's *Book of the Duchess*", *Chaucer Review* 35: 281–93

Bornstein, Diane. "Chaucer's Tale of Melibee as an Example of the Style Clergial", *Chaucer Review* 12 (1978): 236–54

Bowden, Betsy. "Ubiquitous Format? What Ubiquitous Format? Chaucer's *Tale of Melibee* as a Proverb Collection", *Oral Tradition* 17 (2002): 169–207

Bradbury, Nancy Mason. "Chaucerian Minstrelsy: *Sir Thopas, Troilus and Criseyde* and English Metrical Romance", in *Tradition and Transformation in Medieval Romance*, Rosalind Field (ed.). Cambridge: D. S. Brewer, 1999: 115–24

Brewer, Derek. "Chaucer's Poetic Style", in *The Cambridge Chaucer Companion*, Piero Boitani and Jill Mann (eds.). Cambridge: Cambridge University Press, 1986: 85–119

Brewer, Derek. *Geoffrey Chaucer: The Critical Heritage Volume 1, 1385–1837*. London: Routledge, 1978

Brönnimann-Egger, Werner. *The Friendly Reader: Modes of Cooperation Between Eighteenth-Century English Poets and Their Audience.* Tübingen: Stauffenburg, 1991

Bronson, Bertrand H. "The *Book of the Duchess* Re-opened", *PMLA* 67 (1952): 863–81

Bronson, Bertrand H. *In Search of Chaucer.* Toronto: University of Toronto Press, 1960

Brown, Peter. *On the Borders of Middle English Dream Visions.* Oxford: Oxford University Press, 1999

Burrow, J. A. "Chaucer's *Sir Thopas* and *La Prise de Nuevile*", *Yearbook of English Studies* 14 (1984): 44–55

Burrow, J. A. *Ricardian Poetry.* London: Routledge, 1971

Burrow, J. A. "*Sir Thopas*: An Agony in Three Fits", *Review of English Studies* 22 (1971): 54–8

Burton, T. L. "Chaucer's *Tale of Sir Thopas*", *Explicator* 40 (1982): 4

Calabrese, Michael. *Chaucer's Ovidian Arts of Love.* Gainesville, Fl.: University of Florida Press, 1994

Camille, Michael. *The Medieval Art of Love.* New York, NY: Abrams, 1998

Cannon, Christopher. *The Making of Chaucer's English.* Cambridge: Cambridge University Press, 1998

Caxton's Book of Curtesye, Frederick J. Furnivall (ed.). London: EETS ES 3, 1868

Chaucer, Geoffrey. *Troilus and Criseyde, A Facsimile of Corpus Christi College Cambridge MS 61,* M. B. Parkes and Elizabeth Salter (eds. and introduction). Cambridge: D. S. Brewer, 1977: 15–23

Chaucerian and Other Pieces, W. W. Skeat (ed.). Oxford: Clarendon Press, 1897

Cicero. *De Inventione, De Optimo Genere Oratorum and Topica,* H. M. Hubbell (ed. and trans.). Cambridge: Harvard University Press, 1949

Cohen, Jeffrey Jerome. "Diminishing Masculinity in Chaucer's *Tale of Sir Thopas*", in *Masculinities in Chaucer: Approaches to Maleness in the* Canterbury Tales *and* Troilus and Criseyde, Peter G. Beidler (ed.). Cambridge: D. S. Brewer, 1998: 143–55

Coleman, Joyce. *Public Reading and the Reading Public in Late Medieval England and France*. Cambridge: Cambridge University Press, 1996

Colette, Carolyn. "A Closer Look at Seinte Cecile's Special Vision", *Chaucer Review* 10 (1976): 337–49

Colette, Carolyn. "Heeding the Counsel of Prudence: A Context for the Melibee", *Chaucer Review* 29 (1995): 416–33

The Complete Works of Geoffrey Chaucer vol. 1, W. W. Skeat (ed.). Oxford: Clarendon Press, 1899

Condren, Edward I. "The Historical Context of the Book of the Duchess: A New Hypothesis", *Chaucer Review* 5 (1971): 195–212

Condren, Edward I. "Of Deaths and Duchesses and Scholars Coughing in Ink", *Chaucer Review* 10 (1975): 87–95

Connolly, Margaret. "Chaucer and Chess", *Chaucer Review* 29 (1994): 40–4

Cooley, Franklin. "Two Notes on the Chess Terms in *The Book of the Duchess*", *MLN* 63 (1948): 30–5

Cooper, Helen. "Chaucer and Ovid: A Question of Authority" in *Ovid Renewed: Ovidian Influences on Literature and Art from the Middle Ages to the Twentieth Century*, Charles Martindale (ed.). Cambridge: Cambridge University Press, 1988: 71–88

Correale, Robert and Mary Hamel, *Sources and Analogues of the Canterbury Tales I*. Cambridge: Boydell and Brewer, 2002

Crosby, Ruth. "Chaucer and the Custom of Oral Delivery", *Speculum* 13 (1938): 413–32

Crow, Martin M. and Clair C. Olson. *Chaucer Life-Records*. Oxford: Clarendon Press, 1966

Curtius, Ernst Robert. *European Literature and the Latin Middle Ages*, William R. Trask (trans.). New York: Harper & Row, 1953

Dahlberg, Charles. "The Narrator's Frame for *Troilus*", *Chaucer Review* 15 (1990): 85–100

Dahlberg, Charles. *The Romance of the Rose*. Princeton, NJ: Princeton University Press, 1971

Davenport, Tony. *Medieval Narrative: An Introduction*. Oxford: Oxford University Press, 2004

Dean, James. "Artistic Conclusiveness in Chaucer's *Parliament of Fowls*", *Chaucer Review* 21 (1986): 16–25

Delany, Sheila. *The Naked Text: Chaucer's* Legend of Good Women. Berkeley, Calif.: University of California Press, 1994

Delasanta, Rodney. "And of Great Reverence: Chaucer's Man of Law", *Chaucer Review* 5 (1971): 288–310

Donaldson, E. T. "Chaucer the Pilgrim", *PMLA* 69 (1954): 928–36

Donaldson, E. T. "The Ending of Chaucer's *Troilus*", in *Early English and Norse Studies Presented to Hugh Smith*, Arthur Brown and Peter Foote (eds.). London: Methuen, 1963: 26–45

Dronke, Peter. "The Conclusion of *Troilus and Criseyde*", *Medium Ævum* 1964 (33): 47–52

Dubs, Kathleen E. and Stoddard Malarkey. "The Frame of Chaucer's *Parlement*", *Chaucer Review* 13 (1978): 16–24

Dyck, E. F. "Ethos, Pathos, and Logos in *Troilus and Criseyde*", *Chaucer Review* 20 (1986): 169–81

Eckhardt, Caroline. "The Medieval Prosimetrum Genre (from Boethius to *Boece*)", *Genre* 16 (1983): 21–38

Eggebroten, Anne. "Laughter in the *Second Nun's Tale*: A Redefinition of the Genre", *Chaucer Review* 19 (1984): 55–61

Eliot, T. S. "Tradition and the Individual Talent", in *Selected Essays*. New York: Harcourt, 1932: 13–22

The English Works of John Gower, vol. 1. G. C. Macaulay (ed.). London: EETS ES 81, 1901

Finlayson, John. "Definitions of Middle English Romance: Part I", *Chaucer Review* 15 (1980): 44–62

Finlayson, John. "Definitions of Middle English Romance: Part II", *Chaucer Review* 15 (1980): 168–81

Fisher, John. "The Legend of Good Women", in *Companion to Chaucer Studies*, Beryl Rowland (ed.). Oxford: Oxford University Press, 1968: 464–76

Fisher, John. "The Revision of the *Prologue* to the *Legend of Good Women*: An Occasional Explanation", *South Atlantic Bulletin* 43 (1978): 75–84

Foster, Edward E. "Has Anyone Here Read *Melibee*?", *Chaucer Review* 34 (2000): 398–409

Fyler, John. *Chaucer and Ovid*. New Haven, Conn.: Yale University Press, 1979

Gallagher, Joseph. "Theology and Intention in Chaucer's *Troilus*", *Chaucer Review* 7 (1972): 44–66
Garbáty, Thomas J. "The Degradation of Chaucer's 'Geffrey'", *PMLA* 89 (1974): 97–104
Gaylord, Alan. "Chaucer's Dainty 'Dogerel': The 'Elvyssh' Prosody of *Sir Thopas*", *Studies in the Age of Chaucer* 1 (1979): 83–104
Gaylord, Alan. "The Moment of Sir Thopas: Towards a New Look at Chaucer's Language", *Chaucer Review* 16 (1982): 311–29
Gaylord, Alan. "Sentence and Solaas in Fragment VII of the *Canterbury Tales*: Harry Bailly as Horseback Editor", *PMLA* 82 (1967): 226–35
Goodman, Anthony. *John of Gaunt: The Exercise of Princely Power in Fourteenth-Century Europe*. London: Longman, 1992
Green, Dennis. "Orality and Reading: The State of Research in Medieval Studies", *Speculum* 65 (1990): 267–80
Grennen, Joseph. "Saint Cecilia's 'Chemical Wedding': The Unity of the Canterbury Tales, Fragment VIII", *Journal of English and Germanic Philology* 65 (1966): 466–81
Grossi Jr., Joseph L. "The Unhidden Piety of Chaucer's *Seint Cecilie*", *Chaucer Review* 36 (2002): 298–309
Haines, Victor. "Where are Chaucer's 'Retracciouns'?", *Florilegium* 10 (1988–91): 127–49
Hanna, Ralph. *Pursuing History: Middle English Manuscripts and Their Texts*. Stanford: Stanford University Press, 1996
Hansen, Elaine Tuttle. *Chaucer and the Fictions of Gender*. Berkeley, Calif.: University of California Press, 1992
Hansen, Elaine Tuttle. "Irony and the Antifeminist Narrator in Chaucer's *Legend of Good Women*", *Journal of English and Germanic Philology* 82 (1983): 11–31
Hardman, Phillipa. "The *Book of the Duchess* as a Memorial Monument", *Chaucer Review* 28 (1994): 205–15
Harriss, G. L. *Cardinal Beaufort: A Study of Lancastrian Ascendancy and Decline*. Oxford: Clarendon Press, 1988
Haskell, Ann S. "Sir Thopas: The Puppet's Puppet", *Chaucer Review* 9 (1975): 253–61
Herlyn, Anne. "So He Says to Her, He Says, 'Well,' He Says...: Multiple Dialogue Introducers From a Historical Perspective",

in *Historical Discourse Analysis*, Andreas H. Jucker et al. (eds.). Amsterdam: John Benjamins, 1999: 313–30

Hill, John M. "The *Book of the Duchess,* Melancholy and That Eight-Year Sickness", *Chaucer Review* 9 (1974): 35–50

Howard, Donald R. *Chaucer: His Life, His Works, His World.* New York, NY: Ballentine Books, 1987

Howard, Donald R. "Chaucer the Man", *PMLA* 80 (1965): 337–43

Huppé, Bernard. *A Reading of the* Canterbury Tales. Albany, NY: State University of New York Press, 1964

Irvine, Martin. "Medieval Grammatical Theory and Chaucer's *House of Fame*", *Speculum* 60 (1985): 850–76

Isidore of Seville, *Etymologiae,* W. M. Lindsay (ed.). Oxford: Oxford University Press, 1911

Kane, George. *Chaucer and Langland.* London: Athlone Press, 1989

Kealy, Kieran. "Voices of the Tabard: The Last Tales of the Canterbury Tales", in *From Arabye to Engelond: Medieval Studies in Honour of Mahmoud Manzalaoui on His 75th Birthday*, A. E. Christa Canitz and Gernot R. Wieland (eds.). Ottawa: University of Ottawa Press, 1999: 113–29

Kean, P. M. "Chaucer's Dealings with a Stanza of *Il Filostrato* and the Epilogue of *Troilus and Criseyde*", *Medium Ævum* 33 (1964): 36–46

Kelly, Henry. *Chaucer and the Cult of St Valentine.* Leiden: Brill, 1986

Kelly, Henry. "The Genoese Saint and Chaucer's Third of May", *Chaucer Newsletter* 1 (1979): 6–10

Kendrick, Laura. "The *Troilus* Frontispiece and the Dramatization of Chaucer's *Troilus*", *Chaucer Review* 22 (1987): 81–93

Kittredge, George Lyman. *Chaucer and His Poetry.* Cambridge, Mass.: Harvard University Press, 1920

Knight, Stephen. *Geoffrey Chaucer.* Oxford: Blackwell, 1986

Kolve, V. A. *Chaucer and the Imagery of Narrative.* Stanford: Stanford University Press, 1984

Kreuzer, James R. "The Dreamer in the *Book of the Duchess*", *PMLA* 66 (1951): 543–7

Kruger, Stephen. *Dreaming in the Middle Ages.* Cambridge: Cambridge University Press, 1992

Lambert, Mark. "*Troilus*, Books I–III", in *Essays on Troilus and Criseyde*, Mary Salu (ed.). Cambridge: D. S. Brewer, 1979: 105–25

Lassahn, Nicole. "Literary Representations of History in Fourteenth Century England: Shared Technique and Divergent Practice in Chaucer and Langland", *Essays in Medieval Studies* 17 (2000): 49–58

Lawton, David. *Chaucer's Narrators*. Cambridge: D. S. Brewer, 1985

Lawton, David. "Skelton's Use of *Persona*", *Essays in Criticism* 30 (1980): 9–28

Lerer, Seth. *Chaucer and His Readers*. Princeton, NJ: Princeton University Press, 1993

Lewis, C. S. "What Chaucer Really Did to *Il Filostrato*", *Essays and Studies* 17 (1931): 56–75

Lewis, N. B. "The Anniversary Service for Blanche, Duchess of Lancaster, 12th September 1374", *Bulletin of the John Rylands Library* 21 (1937): 3–19

Longsworth, Robert. "Privileged Knowledge: St Cecilia and the Alchemist in the Canterbury Tales", *Chaucer Review* 27 (1992): 87–96

Louis, Cameron. "The Concept of the Proverb in Middle English", *Proverbium* 14 (1997): 173–85

Lumiansky, R. M. "The Bereaved Narrator in Chaucer's the *Book of the Duchess*", *Tennessee Studies in Literature* 9 (1959): 5–17

Lynch, Kathryn L. *Chaucer's Philosophical Visions*. Cambridge: D. S. Brewer, 2000

Major, John M. "The Personality of Chaucer the Pilgrim", *PMLA* 75 (1960): 160–2

Malaczkov, Szilvia. "Geoffrey Chaucer's Translation Strategies", *Perspectives: Studies in Translatology* 9 (2001): 33–44

Manly, John M. *Chaucer and the Rhetoricians*. London: British Academy, 1926

Mann, Jill. *Chaucer and Medieval Estates Satire*. Cambridge: University Press, 1973

Mann, Jill. *Geoffrey Chaucer*. New York, NY: Harvester Wheatsheaf, 1991

Mann, Jill. "Troilus' Swoon", *Chaucer Review* 14 (1980): 319–35

Martin, Priscilla. *Chaucer's Women: Nuns, Wives and Amazons.* Iowa City, Iowa: University of Iowa Press, 1990

Massey, Jeff. "'The *Double Bind* of Troilus to Tellen': The Time of the Gift in Chaucer's *Troilus and Criseyde*", *Chaucer Review* 38 (2003): 16–35

McDonald, Nicola. "Chaucer's *Legend of Good Women*, Ladies at Court and the Female Reader", *Chaucer Review* 35 (2000): 22–42

McDonald, Nicola. *Pulp Fictions of Medieval England: Essays in Popular Romance.* Manchester: Manchester University Press, 2004

Meale, Carol M. "The Compiler At Work: John Colyns and BL MS Harley 2252", in *Manuscripts and Readers in Fifteenth-Century England*, Derek Pearsall (ed.). Cambridge: D. S. Brewer, 1983: 82–103

Meale, Carol M. "The Politics of Book Ownership: The Hopton Family and Bodleian Library, Digby MS 185", in *Prestige, Authority and Power in Late Medieval Manuscripts and Texts*, Felicity Riddy (ed.). Woodbridge: Boydell, 2000: 82–103

Meale, Carol M. and Julia Boffey, "Gentlewomen's Reading", in *Cambridge History of the Book in Britain: Volume III 1400–1557*, Lotte Hellinga and J. B. Trapp (eds.). Cambridge: Cambridge University Press, 1999: 526–40

Mehl, Dieter. "Chaucer's Narrator: Troilus and Criseyde and the Canterbury Tales", in *The Cambridge Chaucer Companion*. Piero Boitani and Jill Mann (eds.). Cambridge: Cambridge University Press, 1986: 213–42

Mehl, Dieter. *Geoffrey Chaucer: An Introduction to his Narrative Poetry.* Cambridge: Cambridge University Press, 1986

Metamorphoses 2 vols, Frank Justus Miller (ed.). Cambridge, Mass.: Harvard University Press, 1946

Miller, Jacqueline. "The Writing on the Wall: Authority and Authorship in Chaucer's *House of Fame*", *Chaucer Review* 17 (1982): 95–115

Minnis, A. J. *Chaucer and Pagan Antiquity.* Cambridge: D. S. Brewer, 1982

Minnis, A. J. *Medieval Theory of Authorship*. London: Scolar Press, 1988

Minnis, A.J. *Oxford Guides to Chaucer: The Shorter Poems*. Oxford: Oxford University Press, 1995: 79–80

Mooney, Linne. "Chaucer's Scribe", *Speculum* 81 (2006): 97–138

Morgan, Gerald. "Moral and Social Identity and the Idea of Pilgrimage in the *General Prologue*", *Chaucer Review* 37 (2003): 285–314

Morse, Ruth. *Truth and Convention in the Middle Ages: Rhetoric, Representation, and Reality*. Cambridge: Cambridge University Press, 1991

Murphy, James J. "A New Look at Chaucer and the Rhetoricians", *Review of English Studies* 14 (1964): 1–20

Murray, H. J. R. *History of Chess*. Oxford: Clarendon Press, 1918

Muscatine, Charles. *Chaucer and the French Tradition*. Berkeley, Calif.: University of California Press, 1957

Nevo, Ruth. "Chaucer: Motive and Mask in the *General Prologue*", *Modern Language Review* 58 (1963): 1–9

Nicholson, Peter. "Chaucer Borrows from Gower: The Sources of the *Man of Law's Tale*", in *Chaucer and Gower: Difference, Mutability, Exchange*, R. F. Yeager (ed.). Victoria: University of Victoria, 1991: 85–99

Nicholson, Peter. "The Man of Law's Tale: What Chaucer Really Owed to Gower", *Chaucer Review* 26 (1991): 153–74

Œuvres complètes de Eustache Deschamps vol. 11, A. H. E. Queux de Saint Hilaire (ed.). Paris: Firmin Didot, 1903

Œuvres de Guillaume de Machaut, 3 vols., Ernest Hoepffner (ed.). Paris: Librairie de Firmin-Didot et Companie, 1921

Olson, Glending. "Chaucer, Dante and the Structure of Fragment VIII (G) of the *Canterbury Tales*", *Chaucer Review* 16 (1982): 222–36

Ong, Walter J. "Oral Residue in Tudor Prose Style", *PMLA* 80 (1965): 145–54

Ong, Walter J. *Orality and Literacy: The Technologizing of the Word*. London: Routledge, 1982

Ong, Walter J. "Orality, Literacy, and Medieval Textualization", *NLH* 16 (1984): 1–12

Ovide moralisé, C. de Boer, (ed.). Amsterdam: Johannes Müller, 1915

Owen Jr., Charles A. "What the Manuscripts Tell Us about the Parson's Tale", *Medium Ævum* 63 (1994): 239–49

Palmer, J. J. N. "The Historical Context of the *Book of the Duchess:* A Revision", *Chaucer Review* 8 (1974): 253–61

Palmer, R. Barton. "The Metafictional Machaut: Self-Reflexivity and Self-Mediation in the Two Judgment Poems", *Studies in the Literary Imagination* 20 (1987): 23–39

Parkes, M. B. "Reading, Copying and Interpreting a Text in the Early Middle Ages", in *A History of Reading in the West*, Guglielmo Cavallo and Roger Chartier (eds.). Cambridge: Polity, 1999: 90–102

Patterson, Lee. "The *Parson's Tale* and the Quitting of the *Canterbury Tales*", *Traditio* 34 (1978): 331–80

Patterson, Lee. "What Man Artow? Authorial Self-Definition in The Tale of Sir Thopas and The Tale of Melibee", *Studies in the Age of Chaucer* 11: 117–75

Payne, Robert O. "Chaucer and the Art of Rhetoric", in *A Companion to Chaucer Studies*, Beryl Rowland (ed.). New York: Oxford University Press, 1979: 42–64

Payne, Robert O. "Making His Own Myth: The *Prologue* to Chaucer's *Legend of Good Women*", *Chaucer Review* 9 (1975): 197–211

Pearsall, Derek. *The Life of Geoffrey Chaucer*. Oxford: Blackwell, 1992

Pearsall, Derek. "Review of John H. Fisher, *The Importance of Chaucer*", *Speculum* 68 (1993): 760–1

Pearsall, Derek. "The *Troilus* Frontispiece and Chaucer's Audience", *Yearbook of English Studies* 7 (1977): 68–74

Peck, Russell A. "The Ideas of 'Entente' and Translation in Chaucer's *Second Nun's Tale*", *Studia Mediaevale* 8: 17–37

Percival, Florence. *Chaucer's Legendary Good Women*. Cambridge: Cambridge University Press, 1998

Polzella, Marion. "'The Craft So Long to Lerne': Poet and Lover in Chaucer's *Envoy to Scogan* and *Parliament of Fowls*", *Chaucer Review* 10 (1976): 279–86

Porter, Pamela F. *Courtly Love in Medieval Manuscripts*. London: British Library, 2003

Quinn, William. *Chaucer's* Rehersynges: *The Performability of The Legend of Good Women*. Washington, D.C.: University Press of America, 1994

Quinn, William. "Medieval Dream Visions: Chaucer's *Book of the Duchess*", in *Readings in Medieval Texts: Interpreting Old and Middle English Literature,* David Johnson and Elaine Treharne (eds.). Oxford: Oxford University Press, 2005: 323–36

Reeves, Compton. *Pleasures and Pastimes in Medieval England*. Oxford: Oxford University Press, 1995

Reiss, Edmund. "Chaucer and Medieval Irony", *Studies in the Age of Chaucer* 1 (1979): 67–82

Robertson, D. W. "The Historical Setting of Chaucer's *Book of the Duchess*", in *Medieval Studies in Honor of Urban Tigner Holmes*, John Mahoney and Jon Esten Keller (eds.). Chapel Hill, NC, 1966: 169–95

Le Roman de la rose, 5 vols, Ernest Langlois (ed.). Paris: Libraire de Firmin-Didot, 1914

Roper, Gregory. "Dropping the Personae and Reforming the Self: The *Parson's Tale* and the End of the *Canterbury Tales*", in *Closure in the Canterbury Tales: The Role of the Parson's Tale*, David Raybin and Linda Tarte Holley (eds.). Kalamazoo, Mich.: Western Michigan University Press, 2000: 151–75

Rosenberg, Bruce A. "The Contrary Tales of the Second Nun and the Canon's Yeoman", *Chaucer Review* 2 (1968): 278–91

Rowland, Beryl. "Chaucer's Duchess and Chess", *Florilegium* 16 (1999): 41–60

Rowney, Ian. "Arbitration in Gentry Disputes of the Later Middle Ages", *History* 67 (1982): 367–74

Sadlek, Gregory M. "Love, Labor, and Sloth in Chaucer's *Troilus and Criseyde*", *Chaucer Review* 26 (1992): 350–67

Salter, Elizabeth. "*Troilus and Criseyde*: Poet and Narrator", in *Acts of Interpretation*, Mary J. Carruthers and Elizabeth D. Kirk (eds.). Norman, Oklahoma: Pilgrim, 1982: 281–91

Scanlon, Larry. *Narrative, Authority and Power: The Medieval Exemplum and the Chaucerian Tradition*, Cambridge: Cambridge University Press, 1994

Scattergood, V. J. "Chaucer and the French War: *Sir Thopas* and *Melibee*", in *Court and Poet*, Glyn S. Burgess (ed.). Liverpool: Cairns, 1981: 287–96

Schlauch, Margaret. "The Art of Chaucer's Prose", in *Chaucer and Chaucerians: Critical Studies in Middle English Literature,* D. S. Brewer (ed.). London: Thomas Nelson and Sons, 1966: 140–63

Schless, Howard. "A Dating for the *Book of the Duchess:* Line 1314", *Chaucer Review* 19 (1985): 272–6

Scott, Kathleen L. "A Mid Fifteenth-Century English Illuminating Shop and its Customers", *Journal of the Warburg and Courtauld Institutes* 31 (1968): 170–96

Seibert, Harriet. "Chaucer and Horace", *MLN* 31 (1916) 304–7

Sell, Roger D. *Literature as Communication*. Amsterdam: John Benjamins, 2000

Severs, J. Burke. "Chaucer's Self-Portrait in the *Book of the Duchess*", *Philological Quarterly* 43 (1964): 27–39

Shannon, Edgar Finley. *Chaucer and the Roman Poets.* Cambridge, Mass.: Harvard University Press, 1929

Shoeck, R. J. "Chaucerian Irony Revisited: A Rhetorical Perspective", *Florilegium* 11 (1992): 124–41

Sir Gawain and the Green Knight, J. R. R. Tolkien, E. V. Gordon and Norman Davis (eds.), 2nd edn. Oxford: Clarendon Press, 1967

Sklute, Larry. "The Inconclusive Form of the *Parliament of Fowls*", *Chaucer Review* 16 (1981): 119–28

Sklute, Larry. *Virtue of Necessity: Inconclusiveness and Narrative Form in Chaucer's Poetry*. Columbus: Ohio State University Press, 1984

Smyth, Karen Elaine. "Reassessing Chaucer's Cosmological Discourse at the End of *Troilus and Criseyde* (c.1385)", *Fifteenth-Century Studies* 32 (2007): 150–63

Spearing, A. C. *The Medieval Poet as Voyeur.* Cambridge: Cambridge University Press, 1993

Spearing, A. C. "A Ricardian 'I': The Narrator of *Troilus and Criseyde*", in *Essays in Ricardian Literature*, A. J. Minnis,

Charlotte C. Morse, and Thorlac Turville-Petre (eds.). Oxford: Clarendon Press, 1997: 1–22

Spearing, A. C. *Textual Subjectivity*. Oxford: Oxford University Press, 2005

Stephens, John. "The Uses of Personae and the Art of Obliqueness in Some Chaucer Lyrics, Part I", *Chaucer Review* 21 (1987): 360–73

Stevens, Martin. "Chaucer's 'Bad Art': The Interrupted Tales", in *The Rhetorical Poetics of the Middle Ages: Reconstructive Polyphony*, John M. Hill and Deborah M. Sinnreich-Levi (eds.). Madison, NJ: Fairleigh Dickinson University Press, 2000: 130–48

Stevenson, Kay Gilliland. "Readers, Poets and Poems within the Poem", *Chaucer Review* 24 (1989): 1–19

Stock, Brian "Medieval Literacy, Linguistic Theory, and Social Organization", *NLH* 16 (1984): 13–29

Strohm, Paul. *Social Chaucer*. Cambridge, Mass.: Harvard University Press, 1989

Taylor, Andrew. "Into His Secret Chamber: Reading and Privacy in Late Medieval England" in *The Practice and Representation of Reading in England*, James Raven et al. (eds.). Cambridge: Cambridge University Press, 1996: 41–61

Taylor, Karla. "Social Aesthetics and the Emergence of Civic Discourse from the Shipman's Tale to Melibee", *Chaucer Review* 39 (2005): 298–322

Turville-Petre, Thorlac. *England the Nation*. Oxford: Oxford University Press, 1996

Vaughan, Míceál F. "Creating Comfortable Boundaries: Scribes, Editors, and the Invention of the *Parson's Tale*", in *Rewriting Chaucer: Culture, Authority, and the Idea of the Authentic Text, 1400–1602*, Thomas A. Prendergast and Barbara Kline (eds.). Columbus: Ohio State University Press, 1999: 45–90

Wack, Mary. *Lovesickness in the Middle Ages: The Viaticum and its Commentaries*. Philadelphia: University of Pennsylvania Press, 1990

Wack, Mary. "Lovesickness in Troilus", *Pacific Coast Philology* 19 (1984): 55–73

Wallace, David. "Chaucer's Continental Inheritance: The Early Poems and *Troilus and Criseyde*", in The *Cambridge Chaucer Companion*, Piero Boitani and Jill Mann (eds.). Cambridge: Cambridge University Press, 1986: 19–37

Wallace, David. *Chaucerian Polity*. Stanford, Calif.: Stanford University Press, 1997

Warren, Victoria. "(Mis)Reading the 'Text' of Criseyde: Context and Identity in Chaucer's *Troilus and Criseyde*", *Chaucer Review* 36 (2001): 1–15

Waswo, Richard. "The Narrator of Troilus and Criseyde", *ELH* 50 (1983): 1–25

Waterhouse, Ruth and Gwen Griffiths. "'Sweete wordes' of Non-Sense: The Deconstruction of the Moral *Melibee* (Part I)", *Chaucer Review* 23 (1989): 338–61

Watson, Robert A. "Dialogue and Invention in the *Book of the Duchess*", *Modern Philology* 98 (2001): 543–76

Weil, Eric. "An Alchemical Freedom Flight: Linking the *Manciple's Tale* to the *Second Nun's* and *Canon's Yeoman's Tales*", *Medieval Perspectives* 6 (1990): 162–70

Weisl, Angela Jane. *Conquering the Reign of Femeny: Gender and Genre in Chaucer's Romance*. Cambridge: D. S. Brewer, 1995

Wetherbee, Winthrop. *Chaucer and the Poets: An Essay on Troilus and Criseyde*. Ithaca, NY: Cornell University Press, 1984

Wetherbee, Winthrop. "'*Per te poeta fui, per te cristiano*': Dante, Statius, and the Narrator of Chaucer's *Troilus*", in *Vernacular Poetics in the Middle Ages*, Lois Ebin (ed.). Kalamazoo, Mich.: Medieval Institute Publications, 1984: 153–76

Wilhelm, James. "The Narrator and His Narrative in Chaucer's *Parlement*", *Chaucer Review* 1 (1967): 201–06

Windeatt, B. A. *Chaucer's Dream Poetry: Sources and Analogues*. Cambridge: D. S. Brewer, 1982

Windeatt, Barry. *Troilus and Criseyde*. Oxford: Oxford University Press, 1992

Wolfe, Matthew C. "Placing Chaucer's *Retraction* for a Reception of Closure", *Chaucer Review* 33 (1999): 427–31

Wolfson, Nessa. *CHP: The Conversational Historical Present in American English Narrative*. Dordrecht: Foris, 1982

Wrenn, C. L. "Chaucer's Knowledge of Horace", *Modern Language Review* 18 (1923): 286–92

Wurtele, Douglas. "The Penitence of Geoffrey Chaucer", *Viator* 11 (1980): 335–61

Zink, Michel. *The Invention of Literary Subjectivity*, David Sices (trans.). Baltimore: Johns Hopkins University Press, 1999

Index

Augustine of Hippo 102–3

Beaufort, John 37
Bernard of Clairvaux 132
Bible 118–19
Blanche, duchess of Lancaster 33–4
Boccaccio 109–10, 111, 117–18
Boethius 103–14, 112–13, 171–2
Book of Curtesye (Caxton's) 12, 30

Caxton, William 13
Chaucer, Geoffrey
   Anelida and Arcite 81–2, 120
   Boece 171–2
   Book of the Duchess 15–16, 82, 84–5, 120, 176, 177
   Canterbury Tales, The 94, 97–105, 163–72, 175–6
   "Complaint of Chaucer to His Purse, The" 42
   "Complaint Unto Pity, The" 20
   "Fortune" 20
   House of Fame, The 87–95, 160, 175, 177
   "Lak of Stedfastnesse" 42
   Legend of Good Women, The 95–6, 120, 123, 135–9, 160
   Parliament of Fowls, The 82–5, 93, 120, 175
   Retraction 27–8, 157–60
   Treatise on the Astrolabe, The 27
   Troilus and Criseyde 19–20, 22, 82, 175–6
   "Wordes unto Adam" 41
Chaucer, Lewis 27

Chaucer, Philippa 44–5
Chess 75–8
Cicero 129
Contemptus mundi 15, 110–12, 176–7
Curtius, Ernst 118–19

Dante 111
Deschamps 11
Dream-theory 88–90

Edward III 34, 36
Eliot, T. S. 18

Ford, Ford Madox 18

Giovanni da Lignano 98
Gower, John 11, 108, 131, 141–2

Henryson, Robert 12, 160–1
Heroism 146–7
Hoccleve, Thomas 12

Isidore of Seville 103, 116

Jacobus de Cessolis 76–7
Jean, duke of Berry 50, 58
John of Gaunt 33–7, 39–40, 42–4, 63, 79–80, 177
John of Montfort 35
John of Wales
   Communeloquium 75

Launfal, Sir 24
Lorris, Guillaume de 13
Lovesickness 45–7, 107

Lydgate, John 12, 124, 160

Machaut, Guillaume de 13, 49–50, 58, 65, 68–9, 73, 177
Marie de France 24
Meun, Jean de 13, 53–5

Narrators, Unreliable 15–20, 81–2, 126–128, 177–8

Orpheus 53–5
Ovid 117, 140–1
 Metamorphoses 49–55, 59–63
 Other works 53, 90
Ovide moralise 56

Petrarch 98
Pinkhurst, Adam 41

Politeness 69–71, 165–6, 172–4, 176
Prelection 23–5, 97–105, 120–1, 124–6, 128–30, 148, 166, 170
 Auto-prelection 24–5, 30–1, 122–4, 149–54, 167–70, 176–8

Rhetoric 11–15, 48, 65–7, 69–70, 90–1, 100–1, 113–15, 118–20, 136–8, 165–8, 176–8
Romance 142–5

Schachzal-Spil 75
Swynford, Katherine 37–8

Usk, Thomas 11

Virgil, 89–91